# FORE

*The Hidden Places* series is a collecti<sub>…</sub> you, in this instance, on a relaxed but informative tour of Somerset. Somerset, a county with an attractive green undulating landscape, is famous for its old wool towns and stone-built villages situated on and around the rivers Frome and Avon.

Our books contain a wealth of interesting information on the history, the countryside, the towns and villages and the more established places of interest in the county. But they also promote the more secluded and little known visitor attractions and places to stay, eat and drink many of which are easy to miss unless you know exactly where you are going.

We include hotels, inns, restaurants, public houses, teashops, various types of accommodation, historic houses, museums, gardens, garden centres, craft centres and many other attractions throughout Somerset, all of which are comprehensively indexed. Most places have an attractive line drawing and are cross-referenced to coloured maps found at the rear of the book. We do not award merit marks or rankings but concentrate on describing the more interesting, unusual or unique features of each place with the aim of making the reader's stay in the local area an enjoyable and stimulating experience.

Whether you are visiting the area for business or pleasure or in fact are living in the county we do hope that you enjoy reading and using this book. We are always interested in what readers think of places covered (or not covered) in our guides so please do not hesitate to use the reader reaction forms provided to give us your considered comments. We also welcome any general comments which will help us improve the guides themselves. Finally if you are planning to visit any other corner of the British Isles we would like to refer you to the list of other *Hidden Places* titles to be found at the rear of the book.

# CONTENTS

# 1 Bath and Northeast Somerset

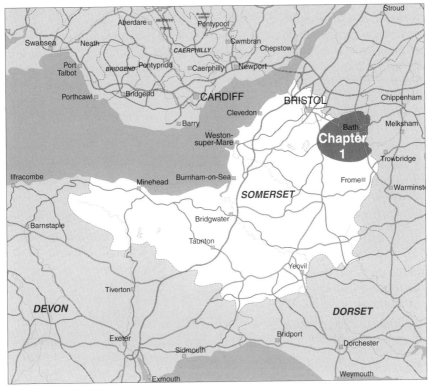

© MAPS IN MINUTES ™ (1998)

## BATH

Bath is of course one of the most remarkable cities in Britain. It is a glorious concoction of architectural set pieces which have been constructed around the only hot thermal springs in the country since the time of the ancient Romans. Best explored on foot, magnificent examples of the city's Roman, medieval or Georgian heritage lie around almost every corner.

Since time immemorial, over half a million gallons of water a day at a constant temperature of 46°C have bubbled to the surface at this point. The ancient Celts believed the mysterious steaming spring was the domain of the goddess Sulis, and it is likely they were aware of its healing properties long before the arrival of the Roman legions in 43AD. However, the Romans were the first to enclose the spring, and within a few short years of their arrival, they had created the spectacular health resort known as *Aquae Sulis*, a name coined as a gesture to the Celtic population they now controlled. Indeed, they even dedicated the temple adjoining the baths to the joint goddess, Sulis-Minerva, to embody both the Celtic and Roman ideologies.

By the 3rd century, Bath had become so renowned that high-ranking soldiers and officials were coming here from all over the Roman world. Public buildings, such as a temple and forum, were added, and the whole city enclosed behind a stone wall. However, by the year 410, the Empire was crumbling and the last remaining legions were forced to return home. Aquae Sulis was abandoned, and within a few decades the drainage systems failed and the marsh returned.

With the possible exception of Hadrian's Wall, the Roman remains at Bath are the most outstanding to survive in Britain. The main reason for their exceptional state of preservation is that for over a thousand years, they remained buried under several feet of dense alluvial mud. Ironically, the ancient baths remained hidden throughout the entire period of Bath's 18th-century renaissance as a spa town and were only rediscovered in the late 19th century; indeed, they were not fully excavated until the 1920s.

The restored remains which can be seen today are centred around the **Great Bath**, a rectangular lead-lined pool which is surrounded by steps and the truncated remains of a colonnaded quadrangle. Five separate phases were constructed over a 200 year period which began in the middle of the 1st century. The result is a superb complex of buildings incorporating swimming pools, mineral baths and a series of chambers heated by underfloor air ducts which would have functioned as saunas and Turkish baths. A

**Royal Baths, Bath**

visit to the Roman Baths includes admission to a fascinating museum of Roman coins, artefacts, jewellery and perhaps the finest exhibit of all, a bronze head of the goddess Sulis Minerva.

The population of Bath fell away during the Dark Ages, and it wasn't until the 8th century that the Saxons founded a nunnery here which put the settlement back on the map. This was later elevated to monastic status when King Edgar of Wessex chose to be crowned "King of all England" here in 973. The present great church was begun in 1499 after its Norman predecessor had been destroyed by fire; however in 1539, Henry VIII's Dissolution of the Monasteries brought work to a halt. The church then had to remain without a roof for three quarters of a century, and indeed, the structure wasn't fully completed until 1901.

With its soaring buttresses, spiky ramparts and vast windows of clear glass, **Bath Abbey** is now considered the ultimate example of English Perpendicular church architecture. Its delicate stone fan-vaulting hangs 70 feet above the nave, and its curious castellated tower is rectangular rather than square because it was built using the pillar-foundations of the earlier building. Inside, there is an unusual 18th century portable oak font and a surprising number of monuments and tablets, more than in any church outside Westminster abbey. Some were erected in memory of the many wealthy invalids who flocked here in the 18th and early 19th centuries and were never well enough to return home.

One tablet in the abbey stands as a memorial to Richard "Beau" Nash, a legendary Bath figure who was one of the three people generally considered responsible for turning Bath into a fashionable Georgian spa town. Prior to Nash's arrival in the first decade of the 1700s, Bath had been a squalid community of around 2000 inhabitants whose former prosperity as a medieval wool town had all but disappeared. Historical accounts tell of farm animals roaming freely within the confines of the old Roman town and sewage running down the streets. Notwithstanding, small numbers of the rich and aristocratic continued to be attracted to Bath for its curative hot spring, and in the mid 17th century, the authorities finally took action to improve sanitary conditions, an initiative which was rewarded in 1702 by a visit from Queen Anne.

The best of French and English cuisine is served at **Tilleys Bistro**, located down one of the characterful tiny alleyways surrounding the Abbey. There are three floors to this distinctive and gracious bistro - basement level, ground floor and first floor lounge/conference room. All three dining areas are cosy, warm and have an informal and relaxed ambience. Proprietors Dave and Dawn Mott are friendly and welcoming hosts who were born and bred in Bath, and have owned this superior bistro since 1991. Dawn looks after front of house, while Dave organises the kitchen and superb menu. Open for lunchtime and candlelit evening meals, the menu offers a great variety of dishes. Diners can choose several options which come in small portions, providing lots of variety without the risk of 'over-indulgence'. All the dishes on the menus are intended to be eaten as starters; guests are free to choose as many as they would like. The accent here is definitely a French one, with delicious choices such as poached salmon, chicken livers in a brandy, Dijon mustard and cream sauce, or crepes. The lunch menu, too, offers a range of meat, seafood/fish and vegetarian dishes, innovatively prepared and presented. There is also a selection of vegetables, potatoes, salads and other extras such as garlic bread. The selection of French and English cheeses or mouthwatering desserts - dairy ice creams, clotted cream bread-and-butter pudding, pecan pie, cheesecake and more - are well worth leaving room for. Discerning diners will appreciated the care and expertise that has gone into preparing all dishes to order. The service is conscientious and friendly, and the pace unhurried at this charming and elegant bistro.

"Beau" Nash was, as his nickname tells us, a man of great elegance and style, and he took upon himself the job of improving the city. Despite

**Tilleys Bistro, 3 North Parade Passage, Bath BA1 1 NX Tel: 01225 484200 e-mail: dmott@tilleysbistro.co.uk website: www.tilleysbistro.co.uk**

having been something of a reprobate himself - he had been a modest failure at Oxford, in the Guards and as a lawyer, and only came to Bath in an attempt to earn his living as a gambler - he rose to become Bath's Master of Ceremonies, an unpaid, yet highly influential position to which he ascended when the previous MC was killed in a duel. He pressurised the corporation into paving, cleaning and lighting the streets, outlawed duelling and the wearing of swords, and set about creating a relaxed social atmosphere in which the gentry (the landed middle-class) could mix on equal terms with their social superiors, the aristocracy. Under his guidance, Bath became elegant and fashionable, and soon began to attract significant numbers of the "right people", not only patrons, but also the architects and entrepreneurs who shared Nash's grand vision for the city. Among these was the architect John Wood who, along with his son (also called John), designed most of the city's finest neoclassical squares and terraces. These included North and South Parades, Queen Square, The Circus, and most notably, **Royal Crescent**, John Wood the Younger's Palladian masterpiece which was the first terrace in Britain to be built to an elliptical design. Bath's third

18th-century founding father was Ralph Allen, an entrepreneur who made his first fortune developing an efficient postal system for the provinces, and who went on to make a second as the owner of the local quarries which supplied most of the honey-coloured Bath-stone to the city's Georgian building sites.

A good place to begin a walk around central Bath is at the **Roman Baths**, whose adjoining **Pump Room** looks much as it did when it was completed in 1796. Now an elegant tearoom, a restorative cup of tea, coffee or spa water can be enjoyed here, often to the accompaniment of live chamber music. Items on show include two sedan chairs, one of which was used as a public taxi by the idle or infirm.

**The County Hotel** was refurbished in 1999 and is easily reached via all main approaches to Bath, being just a five-minute walk from the city centre. There are 22 guest bedrooms ranging from standard rooms to superior with whirlpool, all with the most impressive furnishings, fittings and decor. Owner Maureen Kent, ably assisted by her sister Sandy, takes great pride in running a very friendly and relaxed hotel, and is very conscientious about ensuring that all guests have an enjoyable and restful stay. Sandy manages front of house and reception; Maureen is in charge of every other aspect of this fine hotel, including the kitchen, where her son has contributed to the imaginative breakfast menu,

The County Hotel, 18/19 Pulteney Road, Bath BA2 3EZ
Tel: 01225 425003  Fax: 01225 466493
e-mail: reservations@county-hotel.co.uk
website: www.county-hotel.co.uk

which offer a feast of options. A handsome Reading Room, the Cricket Bar and elegant guests' lounge complete the excellent facilities of this superior hotel.

A short distance away from the Pump Room, the magnificent **Pulteney Bridge** spans the River Avon. The only example of the work of Robert Adam in Bath, it was inspired by Florence's Ponte Vecchio and is the only bridge in Britain to incorporate a terrace of buildings. The nearby weir, with its graceful curving steps, is a superb example of Georgian refinement.

In Bath city centre within easy reach of the railway and coach stations, **Laura Place Hotel** is a gracious and charming Georgian residence. The secluded and secure garden to the rear of the hotel is an oasis of tranquillity. The hotel, and the road on which it is set, is named after Henrietta Laura Pulteney, who was heir to the land around these parts, as a descendant of the Earl of Bath. This superb residence commands a central double-fronted elevation facing a justly famous water fountain. The eight capacious en suite bedrooms have 11-foot ceilings and many original features, and are furnished and decorated with style and comfort in mind. Four rooms have lovely four-poster beds.

**Laura Place Hotel, 3 Laura Place, Great Pulteney Street, Bath BA2 4BH Tel: 01225 463815 Fax: 01225 310222**

The breakfasts are a hearty and delicious start to the day. Proprietor Patricia Bull is a warm and welcoming host, with great style and elegance that is reflected in her superior hotel. No smoking.

Set in beautiful gardens at the end of Great Pulteney Street only 10 minutes' walk from Pulteney Bridge and the centre of the city, the **Holburne Museum** is a jewel in Bath City's crown and one of the finest examples of its elegant Georgian architecture. Originally a spa hotel, the building was adapted for the purposes of a museum by Sir Reginald Blomfield early in the 20th century to house the nucleus of the decorative and fine art collections of Sir William Holburne (1793-1874). On show can be seen superb examples of English and continental silver and porcelain, Italian maiolica and bronzes, together with glass, furniture, miniatures and paintings by such leading English and continental old masters as Gainsborough, Turner, Ramsay, Raeburn and Zoffany. The museum's collection has been added to over the years, with the emphasis remaining on work from the 17th and 18th centuries.

The **Crafts Study Centre** was founded at the Holburne Museum in 1977. This unique establishment incorporates an historic archive of reference books, working notes, documents and photographs relating to leading 20th century

**Holburne Museum, Bath**

artist-craftspeople, along with a permanent exhibition of their work. Items on display include woven and printed textiles, furniture, exquisite calligraphy and ceramics by such artist-potters as Bernard Leach, and also an important collection of work on long-term loan from the Crafts Council. The museum organises a lively programme of events throughout the year, including lectures, concerts and special presentations. In addition, it mounts a series of temporary art and craft exhibitions on a variety of themes, including shows of work by leading contemporary artists and craftspeople. There is also an ongoing education programme, with study facilities being made available for individuals and groups by prior appointment, including access to the extensive library of archive material.

Moving to the north of the area once enclosed by Bath's Roman walls, 40 Gay Street is a place all Jane Austen enthusiasts will not want to miss. Here they will find the **Jane Austen Centre**, opened in 1999. Bath was Austen's home during two long visits here at the end of the 18th century, and she made Bath her home from 1801 until 1806. Her novels *Northanger Abbey* and *Persuasion* are largely set in Bath. The Centre offers visitors a chance to find out more about the Bath of Jane Austen's time and the importance of the city to her life and work. The Centre shop has an unrivalled selection of Jane Austen related books, cards and specially designed gifts.

Gay Street leads through Queen Square to The Circus, a striking example of neoclassical unity of design which is divided into three evenly-proportioned blocks of 11 houses. The street to the northeast leads to the National Trust-owned **Assembly Rooms**, one of the places polite 18th-century society used to congregate to dance, play cards or just be seen. The building was severely damaged during the Second World War and wasn't reopened until 1963. It is now leased to the Bath and North Somerset Council and incorporates an interesting **Museum of Costume.**

**Radnor Guest House** in Bath is a distinguished residence built some 120 years ago. The eye-catching front garden greets visitors with a riot of colour in warmer months; the guest house was awarded a Bath in Bloom award in 1999. There are four en suite guest bedrooms (two doubles, one twin and one family room). The accommodation is spacious and beautifully furnished and decorated. Guests are assured comfort here. The atmosphere is warm, relaxed and informal, so that the guest house feels like a real home from home. There's a variety of options available for breakfast, all delicious and expertly prepared and cooked. Owner Jane Briggs is a conscientious and welcoming host who makes every effort to ensure that all her guests have a pleasant and enjoyable stay. Many of her guests return again and again for her unique brand of warm hospitality.

**Radnor Guest House, 9 Pulteney Terrace, Pulteney Road, Bath, Somerset BA2 4HJ Tel: 01225 316159 Fax: 01225 319199 e-mail: radnorguesthouse@bath10.freeserve.co.uk**

**Membland Guest House** presents an eye-catching and welcoming face to the world, with its flower-filled front garden and impressive Victorian exterior. Owner Peter Moore bought this interesting terraced house in 1982, and has since restored and refurbished throughout while retaining the original late-19th-century style and character. A trained design engineer, his experience, taste and flair are reflected throughout this gracious guest house. Central for all of Bath's sights, and within reach of the railway station, guests can if they wish can be collected from the station on their arrival and brought to the guest house. There are three charming en suite guest bedrooms, each very comfortable and spacious, decorated and furnished with considerable elegance and exquisite design

**Membland Guest House, 7 Pultney Terrace,
Pultney Road, Bath, Somerset BA2 4HJ
Tel: 07958 599572/01225 336712**

ideas, evident throughout the house. Breakfast offers a variety of delicious options.

The street leading west from the Circus leads to **Royal Crescent**, a superb architectural set piece which is popularly regarded as the climax of Palladian achievement in this most classical of English cities. Built between 1767 and 1774 on a site which then overlooked unspoilt countryside, its huge sweep comprises 30 houses, each of which is divided by a giant Ionic half column. No. 1 Royal Crescent has been meticulously restored to its original Georgian splendour by the Bath Preservation Trust.

Although the facades of Bath's Georgian houses were strictly controlled, the internal structure was left to the discretion of their individual owners, many of whom had very different ideas. The result is a fascinating jumble of contrasting masonry, narrow alleys, tradespeople's entrances and eccentric guttering - a half-hidden world which is well worth an inspection.

**Royal Crescent, Bath**

Just along Upper Church Street leading off the Royal Crescent and on to Julian Road, **The Bath Industrial Heritage Centre** offers visitors an insight into the life and times of Mr Jonathan Burdett Bowler, who started his business in Bath in 1872 and described his trade as engineer, brass founder, gasfitter, locksmith and bell-hanger. The business closed in 1969, but remarkably had survived up until this time with its original machinery, Victorian gaslight and everything just as it was nearly 100 years before.

Just a mile from the Royal Crescent in the centre of Bath, along the A431, **Cranleigh** is a charming guest house offering excellent accommodation. The "Mendip Way" walk runs nearby, and it is central for exploring not just Bath but all the sights and attractions of the surrounding area. The residence dates back some 100 years and is built of traditional materials. To the rear there are lovely south-facing cultivated gardens, an oasis of peace and relaxation. There are eight spacious en suite guest bedrooms, individually furnished and decorated with style and comfort in mind. One room has a four-poster, another a distinctive canopied bed. Five rooms offer stunning views over Bath and the Avon valley. The guests' lounge and breakfast room are also handsomely appointed. Interesting objets d'art, high ceilings and the original fireplaces add to the character of this elegant guest house. Breakfast offers a variety of delicious and expertly prepared and presented options. Owners Tony and Jan Poole are conscientious and welcoming hosts. Weekend short breaks are a speciality at this superior guest house. No smoking.

**Cranleigh, 159 Newbridge Hill, Bath, BA1 3PX**
**Tel: 01225 310197  Fax: 01225 423143**
**e-mail: cranleigh@btinternet.com**
**website: www.bath.org/hotel/cran.htm**

The old streets and buildings of Bath are said to be inhabited by an unusual number of ghosts. Two of the most infamous are the Grey Lady, whose characteristic jasmine scent has been detected around the **Theatre Royal** and nearby Garrick's Head inn, and the Black-hatted Man, who is said to appear in and around the Assembly Rooms. Details of a guided Ghost Walk can be obtained from the Tourist Information Centre.

In the exclusive shopping precinct known as Shires Yard in the centre of Bath, **Porter Design** is a distinguished and distinctive fine arts emporium offering a superb range of prints, hand-made frames, cards, decoupage and a host of other exquisite pieces which will add elegance to any home and make for charming and original gifts. The prints themselves cover a vast range of subjects, from stunning floral studies and botanical prints, which number among the shop's specialities, to architectural subjects, costume and figurative works, examples of English naive style, marine landscapes, and ornithological and zoological subjects, covering a range of historical periods, styles and tastes in art over the years. The hand-crafted frames can be chosen to suit a selected fine art print. The hand-carved frames can be hand-gilded, moulded and in various other ways styled according to the customer's wishes. The luxury of hand-crafting means

**Porter Design, 12 Shires Yard, Milsom Street, Bath  BA1 2TD  Tel/Fax: 01225 447261**

that each frame is unique and can be created according to individual specifications. Artists whose prints and cards are sold exclusively here include David Roberts, Lucy Neil (wonderful, decorative still lifes with tulips and honey bees) and Richard Doyle (delightful illustrations of Fairies). Flora and fauna come to life in the handsome and striking prints available here, which will appeal to all discerning visitors. The shop is well laid out for viewing the many prints and other decorative items on sale, and owners Henry and Mary Porter are conscientious and knowledgeable guides to the many lovely wares the shop has to offer. Prices are very reasonable. To add that distinctive touch to any room, this excellent shop should not be missed.

Bath contains an exceptional number of fine art galleries and specialist museums. The **Victoria Art Gallery** near Pulteney Bridge is the city's principal venue for major touring exhibitions. It also has a permanent collection of classical paintings and a smaller gallery displaying work from the area. The **British Folk Art Collection** (formerly the Museum of English Naive Art) in the Paragon is an absorbing anthology of 18th and 19th-century paintings which are characterised by their "direct simplicity". On the same site is the Building of **Bath Museum**, a fascinating collection of models, drawings and illustrations which chronicle the city's unique architectural evolution. **The Museum of East Asian Art** on Bennett Street has a superb collection of Chinese, Japanese, Korean and Southeast Asian artefacts, ranging in date from 5000 BC to the 20th century, all housed in a restored Georgian building. The William Herschel Museum pays tribute to the distinguished 18th century astronomer, who discovered the planet Uranus in 1781, here in what was his home, a delightful period house, with displays of his many achievements - and those of his sister Caroline - and their impact on modern science.

The first recorded mailing of a Penny Black postage stamp was made in 1840 at No. 8 Broad Street, now the site of the **Bath Postal Museum**; exhibits include a reconstruction of a Victorian sorting office and a children's activity room. **Sally Lunn's House** in North Parade Passage is thought to be the oldest house in Bath. Its cellar museum contains the kitchen used by the celebrated 17th-century cook who is attributed with inventing the Bath bun.

Close to Weston on the northern edge of Bath, the ground rises onto Lansdown, a spur of downland which is the site of one the most remarkable follies in Britain. **Beckford's Tower** was built in the 1820s by the wealthy and eccentric scholar, William Beckford, to house his extensive art collection. Crowned by a lantern based on the Lysicrates monument in Athens, the pavilion and bell tower are a wonderful combination of Tuscan, Roman, Greek and Byzantine influences. Visitors climbing the 156 steps to the belvedere are rewarded with a magnificent view stretching from Wiltshire Downs in one direction to the Black Mountains of Wales in the other. There is also a small museum charting Beckford's extraordinary life in pictures, prints and models.

Another of Bath's follies, **Sham Castle**, was constructed on a hill to the east of the city by the quarry-owner Ralph Allen. Built to be seen from his town house, as its name suggests it is merely a romantic facade which is made even more picturesque by night-time illumination. Later in his career, Allen moved out to Prior Park, an ostentatious country mansion on the southeastern edge of Bath which now houses a co-educational school. Designed in classic Palladian style by John Wood the Elder, the house stands within impressive landscaped grounds whose ornamental lakes and superb neoclassical bridge were created under the guidance of Capability Brown and the poet Alexander Pope. The garden enjoys magnificent views.

The National Trust owns 560 acres of countryside and woodland which together form the magnificent **Bath Skyline Walk**. Described in a leaflet obtainable from the National Trust shop in the Abbey Churchyard, the eight-mile footpath offers some spectacular views of Bath's Georgian outline. The route starts above Bathwick to the east of the city and also takes in an Iron Age fieldsystem.

**Ravenscroft** is an elegant Victorian residence with a wealth of period detail. Guests can be assured of a warm welcome amid luxurious surroundings. Within easy reach of Bath city centre, just two to three minutes away, this gracious and appealing hotel is set in an acre of mature, landscaped gardens and occupies an elevated position, affording stunning veiws over Bath and the surrounding countryside. There are four lovely guest bedrooms (three doubles and one single). Two rooms are en suite; two have private bath. Spacious and superbly appointed, the rooms are furnished to a very high standard of comfort and quality. The bountiful and delicious traditional full English breakfast sets guests up for a day's sightseeing or a leisurely walk through the beautiful adjacent countryside. Owners Patrick and Hilary Bryan are amiable and welcoming hosts, who take pleasure in providing excellent service to all their guests. No smoking.

**Ravenscroft, North Road, Bathwick, Bath, Somerset BA2 6HZ Tel/Fax: 01225 461919 e-mail: ravenscroft@compuserve.com website: www.ravenscroftbandb.co.uk**

**Holly Lodge** is an impressive and distinguished Victorian town house offering superior accommodation. Set in its own grounds and gardens, it commands superb views over the gracious city centre of Bath. Rescued from semi-dereliction by George Hall and Carolle Sellick, it was refurbished with taste and style, while remaining in keeping with its origins and date of construction. It retains several period features. There are seven marvellous en suite guest bedrooms (six doubles and one single), designed with an eye for style, colour and coordinates, and offering a high standard of luxury and comfort. Some rooms have queen-size beds; others have four-posters. All have luxury bathrooms and all the other amenities today's discerning guests have come to expect. The guests' lounge is also beautifully furnished and decorated. The imaginative and delicious breakfasts are served in the lovely conservatory breakfast room. In the evenings, guests are welcome to use the floodlit gazebo. Conveniently placed for touring the wide

**Holly Lodge, 8 Upper Oldfield Park, Bath, Somerset BA2 3JZ**
**Tel: 01225 424042 Fax: 01225 481138**
**e-mail: stay@hollylodge.co.uk**
**website: www.hollylodge.co.uk**

range of attractions in the area - apart from the charms of Georgian Bath itself, Wells, Stonehenge, the Cotswolds, the Mendip Hills, South Wales and many other exciting and interesting sights are within a 40-mile radius - this excellent residence makes a wonderful base for exploring the surrounding region. Guests will also welcome the opportunity to relax in the grounds, or take advantage of the opportunities offered by the nearby golf course, riding stables and health spa. Proprietor George Hall and his friendly, conscientious staff take pride in offering the highest standard of service to all their guests. Numerous accolades have been given to this spacious and elegant guest house. No smoking. No pets.

The Combe Down area of Bath was once a village in its own right. Stone quarries and coal mines could be found here; the stone was used not just for local properties but in the construction of Buckingham Palace. **The King William IV** public house was once host to the king whose name it bears. It was built in the 1700s and overlooks a lovely valley. This old staging inn has a great deal of character. The L-shaped main bar area is comfortable and has a relaxed ambience. Prints and old photographs of local scenes adorn the walls. Apart from the excellent range of ales, wines and spirits, the pub also offers tasty home-cooked traditional meals including pies, sandwiches, beef and chicken dishes and more. This attractive and welcoming inn also provides three cosy and comfortable

**The King William IV, 54 Combe Road, Combe Down,
Bath BA2 5HY Tel: 01225 833137**

guest bedrooms (one double, two twins) which have been newly refurbished
and are well furnished and decorated.

## AROUND BATH

BATHEASTON                                        Map 3 ref I2
2 miles NE of Bath on the A4

The A4 to the northeast of Bath leads to Batheaston, a dormitory village above
and to the west of which lies **Little Solsbury Hill**. This 625-foot flat-topped
knoll is topped by a three-sided Iron Age hill fort, one of the simplest and earliest examples of its kind in the country. Excavations have shown that it was
once encircled by a palisade, a sturdy fence made of wooden stakes driven into
the ground which was built onto a low bank faced with dry stone walling.

BATHFORD                                          Map 3 ref I2
2 miles E of Bath on the A363

Another residential community which once belonged to Bath Abbey, Bathford,
is situated a mile to the southeast of Batheaston. Among the many fine 18th-
century buildings to be seen here is **Eagle House**, a handsome residence which
takes its name from the great stone eagle which stands with wings outstretched
on the low-pitched gabled roof. At one time, the old redbrick paper mill by the
river specialised in making paper for bank notes. The tall Italianate tower on
the hill above Bathford is known as **Brown's Folly**. It was built following the
Napoleonic Wars to provide local craftspeople with employment during the

economic depression of the 1830s. The steep path leading up to the folly through Mountain Wood turns into an attractive nature trail along the way

Those travelling between Bathford and Bathampton on the opposite bank of the River Avon have to pay a small toll to cross the bridge. Although only a couple of miles from the centre of Bath, Bathampton's attractive grouping of canal, bridge, church and pub create their own distinct atmosphere. The last-named, the George, is a part 17th-century canalside inn which still has an external door in both its road and towpath sides. Viscount du Barry, the loser of the last legal duel to be fought in England (many illegal ones followed), was brought here following the ill-fated contest on nearby Bathampton Down. The unfortunate viscount died soon after and was buried in the nearby churchyard. According to local legend, however, his ghost has yet to be laid to rest and continues to haunt the inn.

## BATHAMPTON
MAP 3 REF I2
1 mile E of Bath on the A36

Bathampton church is also the final resting place of Admiral Arthur Phillip, the first governor of New South Wales who took the initial shipload of convicts to the colony and established the settlement of Sydney. Considered by some to be the founder of modern Australia (although one would suspect the aboriginal population might not agree), a chapel in the south aisle which already contained memorials to the admiral's family was rechristened the "Australian Chapel" in the 1970s. Bathampton Down above the village is crowned by an ancient hill fort which, according to some historians, was the site of the 6th-century Battle of Badon in which the forces of King Arthur inflicted a crushing defeat on the Saxons.

## CLAVERTON
MAP 3 REF I3
2 miles E of Bath on the A36

The ostentatious tomb of Ralph Allen, the quarry-owning co-founder of 18th-century Bath, lies in the churchyard at Claverton, a pleasant linear village lying on a loop off the A36, a mile to the southeast of Bathampton. The church itself is an unremarkable Victorian reconstruction whose most notable feature is a panel of 14th-century stained glass in the north transept. Six years before his death in 1764, Allen bought **Claverton Manor**, a 16th-century country mansion which was later demolished leaving only a series of overgrown terraces with impressive stonework balustrades. Some of the stone from the ruined house was used to construct the present manor on the hill above the village. The building was designed in elegant neoclassical style by Sir Jeffrey Wyatville, whose work is much in evidence at Windsor Castle, and is set in superb landscaped grounds.

Sir Winston Churchill is reputed to have made his first political speech at Claverton Manor in 1897; however, it is as the **American Museum and Gardens** that the building and grounds are now best known. This absorbing museum was founded in 1961 by Americans Dallas Pratt and John Judkyn and is the only

**American Museum & Gardens, Claverton**

establishment of its kind outside the United States. The rooms have been furnished to show the gradual changes in American living styles, from the arrival of the Pilgrim Fathers in 17th century New England to the Philadelphia and New York of the 18th and 19th centuries. The adobe walls and religious images in the New Mexico Living room give a flour of the life of the Spanish colonists. There is also a large section devoted to the history of Native Americans and a display dedicated to the Shakers. In the Folk Art Gallery, paintings, metalwork and wood carvings demonstrate the diversity and vibrancy of American Folk Art. The Mount Vernon Garden is a replica of George Washington's flower garden at his home in Mount Vernon, Virginia. Throughout the summer months the museum hosts a number of events including displays of Native American dancing and 18th century military drills.

## WESTWOOD

6 miles SE of Bath off the A36

MAP 3 REF I3

Between Bath and Bradford on Avon, **The Peto Garden** at **Ilford Manor** is a Grade I listed Italian-style garden famed for its tranquil beauty. This unique hillside garden was the creation of architect and landscape gardener Harold Peto, who lived here from 1899 until 1933. Steps, terraces, sculpture and magnificent views characterise this superb garden.

The narrow river valley between Bath and Bradford on Avon is shared by the A36, the main railway line and the Kennet and Avon Canal. For around two centuries, water has been mechanically transferred to the canal from the River Avon at the impressive **Claverton Pumping Station**. A mile further south, the canal makes a spectacular diversion over both river and railway by way of the **Dundas Aqueduct**, an impressive Bath stone structure which is finished in characteristic neoclassical style.

Designed by the great engineer, John Rennie, the **Kennet and Avon Canal** was constructed between 1794 and 1810 to link the Thames with the Bristol Avon via Newbury and Devizes. A costly and ambitious project, much of its 75 mile length had to be cut through permeable rock which had to be lined with clay. The enterprise nevertheless succeeded in paying its investors a small dividend before the Great Western Railway arrived in 1841 to poach all its business.

In recent years, the Kennet and Avon Canal Trust has done much to restore this historic waterway, and it is now fully navigable between Bath and Caen Hill near Devizes. For those interested in joining a guided canal trip, narrowboats set out at regular intervals from Sydney Wharf and Bath's Top Lock. Alternatively, small electrically-powered self-drive boats are available from a variety of places including the Dundas Aqueduct.

## HINTON PRIORY                              Map 3 ref I3
4 miles S of Bath off the B3110

Two and a half miles south of the Dundas Aqueduct, the A36 passes close to the atmospheric ruins of **Hinton Priory**, an early Carthusian monastery which was founded in 1232 by Ela, Countess of Salisbury. As in other monastic houses belonging to this order, it was the practice for monks to occupy their own small dwellings which were set around the main cloister, often with tiny gardens attached. The community was generally known for its reclusiveness; however, one outspoken monk, Nicholas Hopkins, achieved notoriety in Tudor times as the confessor and spiritual adviser to 3rd Duke of Buckingham. As recounted by Shakespeare in *Henry VIII*, the so-called "devil monk" told Buckingham he would accede to the throne of England, an unfortunate prophecy which led to the Duke being executed and the monk being imprisoned in the Tower of London. Several sections of the old priory remain, including the chapter house, with its library and dovecote above, the undercroft of the refectory, and parts of the guest quarters.

## HINTON CHARTERHOUSE                        Map 3 ref I3
5 miles S of Bath on the B3110

One mile southwest of Hinton Priory, the **Church of St John the Baptist** at Hinton Charterhouse predates the priory by a century or so. Although much altered, the font, south doorway and lower part of the tower survive from the original Norman structure.

The **Rose & Crown** sits at the heart of the village of Hinton Charterhouse. Locals and discerning visitors from near and far come to sample the delights of this excellent pub. A relaxed atmosphere pervades this traditional pub, with its Tudor-style panelled walls, open fires and collections of large porcelain dinner plates, earthenware jugs and cigarette cards adorning the walls. Owners Paul and Rosemary Harris are warm, welcoming and friendly hosts. The wonderful

**Rose & Crown, High Street, Hinton Charterhouse, Bath BA3 6AN Tel: 01225 722153**

Bath stone fire surround boasts carved busts of Rosemary on one side and Paul on the other - a humourous and yet dignified centrepiece to the main bar. The separate restaurant area is tastefully decorated and very comfortable. The beer garden is lush and well laid out, with formal lawns, shrubs and plenty of tables and chairs for guests to sit and enjoy a quiet drink and some of the superb food on offer. Everything from snacks and sandwiches to hearty steaks, rack of lamb, fresh local trout and much more. Accommodation is soon to be available in the form of four charming and comfortable en suite guest bedrooms (doubles and twins), scheduled to be ready for mid-2000.

## WELLOW
MAP 3 REF H3
4 miles S of Bath off the A367

An undulating lane to the west of Hinton Charterhouse leads to the attractive village of Wellow. A stroll down the main street reveals some fine old houses, a raised walkway, and a charming circular dovecote which is believed to date from the 13th century. The part 14th century church of St Julian contains a unique series of wall paintings dating from around 1500 depicting Christ and the 12 Apostles. On the southern edge of the village, the road descends steeply to a ford on the **Wellow Brook**, beside which stands a handsome medieval packhorse bridge and an old mill, now a private residence. Wellow is also the location of a first-rate pony trekking centre which offers a selection of rides for people of all ages and abilities.

One of the finest examples of a Neolithic long barrow in the west of England can be found beside the road to Shoscombe, three quarters of a mile to the southwest of Wellow. **Stoney Littleton** is a striking multi-chambered tomb which was originally constructed over 4,000 years ago. Now restored, the interior can be inspected by obtaining a key from nearby Stoney Littleton Farm (you are advised to take a torch and clothes you don't mind getting muddy).

## PRISTON

MAP 3 REF H3

4 miles SW of Bath off the B3115

The church tower at Priston is crowned with a disproportionately-large weathercock which was presented to the parish by the local lord of the manor in 1813 as a flamboyant gift. The earliest record of **Priston Mill**, on the northern edge of the village, occurs in the Domesday book of 1086. It has continued to supply flour to the people of the city of Bath ever since. Powered by a spectacular 25 foot overshot water wheel, the millstones still produce genuine stoneground flour for retail sale. Visitors to the mill can learn about its operation and history, or take a trailer ride around the adjoining working farm. The site also incorporates an award-winning nature trail and adventure play area.

## PEASEDOWN ST JOHN

MAP 3 REF H3

5 miles SW of Bath on the A367

Continuing westwards across the A3062, the area incorporating Peasedown St John and Radstock once stood at the heart of the now almost-forgotten Somerset coalfield. Although coal from the margins of the Mendip Hills had been extracted since the 1300s, it was during the 19th century that mining activities got underway in earnest. Indeed, the only building in Peasedown St John prior to 1817 had been the Red Post Inn, still a pleasant pub. The Braysdown colliery opened nearby in the 1820s and soon after, the deepest mine in the area was sunk at Camerton, a couple of miles to the west. Conditions underground were exceptionally hard. Miners often had to operate in seams which were only a couple of feet thick, their only equipment being a pick, a shovel, and a low sledge onto which the coal was loaded for removal. The coalfield began to decline after the First World War and the last colliery at Kilmersdon closed in the 1970s. Visitors now have to look hard to find evidence of this once-thriving industry which at one time employed over 6,000 people and produced over a million tons of coal a year. Some of the now-landscaped spoil heaps can still be recognised as such, and there are also traces of the successive transport systems (canal, then tramway, then rival railways) which were constructed to take the newly-mined coal to market. In recent decades, the former mining communities, which include Paulton and Timsbury, have had to reinvent themselves as dormitory settlements for Bath and Bristol. Together they have little to offer the casual visitor, except for those with an interest in industrial archeology.

## CAMERTON

MAP 3 REF H3

5 miles SW of Bath off the A367

As well as having contained the deepest mine in the area, the ancient community of Camerton has had a long and colourful history. The village stands beside the **Fosse Way**, the great Roman highway which linked the Channel coast near Exeter with the North Sea near Lincoln, and during the 400 year Roman occupation, the settlement was an important metal smelting centre which produced pewter, bronze and iron for the Roman Empire. The site of the Roman settlement lay to the southwest of the present day village, but has now completely disappeared. In the early 19th century, the rector of Camerton was the well-meaning but tormented John Skinner, a man whose life was made a living hell by the conflicting demands of his children, his congregation, the local gentry, miners, mine owners, farmers and rival denominations. In his personal journal, all 98 volumes of which are now in the British Museum, he declared he "would bear testimony that Camerton folk were as bad as the inhabitants of Sodom and Gomorrah". Unable to stand it any longer, he eventually took his own life in the woods beside the rectory. During the 1950s, the local branch line, which is now long gone, was used for filming the classic Ealing comedy, The Titfield Thunderbolt. Lying in the lanes to the west of Camerton, the **Radford Farm and Shire Horse Stable** is an open farm which retains the traditional farming methods of the 1940s and 1950s.

## MIDSOMER NORTON
8 miles SW of Bath on the A362

MAP 3 REF H3

A memorial to the 12 miners killed in an accident at Wellsway coal works in 1839 can be found on the western edge of the St John the Baptist's churchyard in Midsomer Norton. According to the inscription, the men plummeted to their deaths as they were being lowered down the mine shaft when the rope holding the cage "was generally supposed to have been maliciously cut". A pleasant mixture of the old and new, Midsomer Norton's excellent shopping facilities blend attractively with its Georgian houses, 12th-century priory house, and late-medieval tithe barn, an imposing building which was converted into a Roman Catholic church in the early 20th century.

Although the history of the area is one of mining, with coal being hewn from nearby **Norton Hill** until as recently as the 1970s, it is hard to imagine that the beautiful surrounding countryside may once have been strewn with coal tips. Today, the sights and sounds of the colliery have been replaced by open farmland, wild flowers and bird song.

The interesting **Radstock, Midsomer Norton and District Museum** is housed in a converted 18th-century barn at Haydon, a short distance from the Centurion Hotel. Devoted to the people of the North Somerset coalfield, it contains a unique collection of artefacts and photographs which tell the story of the local mines, railways, farms and schools.

## CAMELEY
9 miles SW of Bath off the A37

MAP 3 REF H3

One of the most exceptional church interiors in the area can be found in Cameley, an attractive village which lies to the west of the A37 Bristol-Shepton Mallet road, four miles west of Camerton. The building was referred to by John Betjeman as "Rip Van Winkle's Church" because of the remarkable series of medieval wall paintings which lay undiscovered behind several centuries of whitewash until the 1960s. The murals are believed to have been painted between the 11th and 17th centuries and feature such diverse images as the foot of a giant St Christopher stepping through a fish and crab-infested river, a charming 14th century jester complete with harlequin costume and belled cap, and a rare coat of arms of Charles I.

The two large artificial lakes lying in the northern foothills of the Mendips to the west of Cameley form an area which is sometimes referred to as the region's lake district. Originally constructed to supply Bristol with fresh water, they also provide a first-rate recreational amenity. The smaller **Blagdon Lake** was completed in 1899 and the **Chew Valley Lake** in 1956. Together they have around 15 miles of shoreline and attract visitors from a wide area who come to fish, take part in watersports activities, or observe the wide variety of waterfowl and other birdlife which are attracted to this appealing habitat.

# 2 Bristol and Northwest Somerset

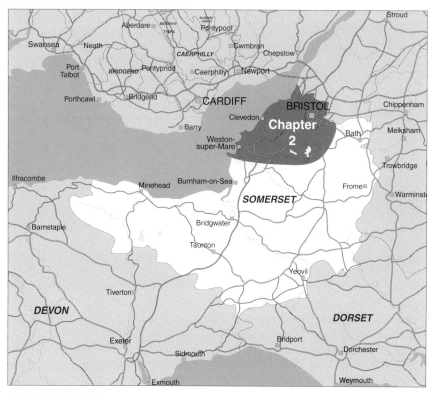

© MAPS IN MINUTES ™ (1998)

## BRISTOL

With a population of over 400,000 and a history dating back to the time of the Saxons, Bristol is a diverse regional capital which takes time to get to know. A good place for the visitor to begin is **Brandon Hill**, an area of open ground near the city centre which can be found to the west of the Park Street shopping area. Here, visitors can climb to the top of the **Cabot Tower**, a 100 foot monument standing near the site of a chapel dedicated to St Brendan the Navigator which was erected in memory of another maritime pioneer, John Cabot. The first non-Scandinavian European to set foot on Newfoundland, Cabot's expedition of 1497 was financed by local Bristol merchants.

For centuries, Bristol was a major commercial seaport, and the magnificent view from the top of the tower reveals a complex series of docks and wharves along a curving stretch of water known as the **Floating Harbour**. This semi-artificial waterway was created when the course of the River Avon was diverted to the south early in the 19th century. A massive feat of civil engineering, the

**Bristol Harbour**

work took over five years to complete and was largely carried out by Napoleonic prisoners using only picks and shovels. Today, the main docks have moved downstream to Avonmouth and the Floating Harbour has become home to a wide assortment of recreational and smaller working craft.

Bristol was founded during Saxon times at the point where the curving River Frome joined the River Avon. This strategically important bridging point at the head of the Avon gorge soon became a major port and market centre, and by the early 11th century the town had its own mint and was trading with other ports throughout western England, Wales and Ireland. In 1067, the Normans began to build a massive stone keep on a site between the present day Floating Harbour and Newgate, a place which is still known as **Castle Park** despite the almost total demolition of the structure at the end of the English Civil War. The heart of the old city lies west of here, around the point where Corn, Broad, Wine and High Streets converge.

Half a mile further west, **Bristol Cathedral** stands at the foot of Park Street on College Green. Founded in about 1140 by Robert Fitzhardinge as the great church of an Augustinian abbey, several original Norman features remain, including the southeast transept walls, chapter house, gatehouse and east side of the abbey cloisters. Elsewhere there is some good 14th century stained glass and a series of striking roof bosses in the north transept. Following the Dissolution of the Monasteries in 1539, Henry VIII took the unusual step of elevating the church to the status of cathedral, and soon after, the richly-carved choir stalls were added. This was followed over a century later by Grinling Gibbons' superbly carved organ case.

The structure wasn't fully completed until the 19th century when a new nave was built in sympathetic style to the existing choir . This now contains some exceptional monuments and tombs, along with a pair of unusual candlesticks which were donated in 1712 by the rescuers of Alexander Selkirk, the actual castaway on whom Daniel Defoe's character, Robinson Crusoe, was modelled.

During the Middle Ages, Bristol expanded enormously as a trading centre and at one time it was second only to London as a seaport. This medieval trade was built on the export of raw wool and woollen cloth from the Mendip and Cotswold Hills and the import of wines from Spain and southwest France. The city's first major wharf development was carried out at this time - the diverting of the River Frome from its original course into the wide artificial channel now known as **St Augustine's Reach**. A remarkable achievement for its day, the excavation created over 500 yards of new berthing and was crucial for Bristol's developing economy.

The city's increasingly wealthy merchants founded one of the most impressive parish churches in the west of England during this period. Originally set in a suburb to the east of the main channel, the church of St Mary Redcliffe is a wonderful arrangement of pinnacles, flying buttresses and sweeping stained glass windows. Queen Elizabeth I called it "the fairest, goodliest and most famous Parish Church in England". Its soaring 290 foot spire is a 19th century addition to the original 13th century tower, and its ornately decorated north porch was built to an unusual hexagonal design which is reputed to have been influenced by the architecture of China. John Cabot is commemorated in the church, and in the south transept Admiral Sir William Penn, whose son William founded the state of Pennsylvania in the US, is buried. An unusual roof boss in the shape of a circular maze can be seen in the north aisle. A giant replica of this, complete with water channels and raised walkways, can be seen in **Victoria Park**, half a mile away to the south. The sandstone beneath St Mary Redcliffe is riddled with underground passages known as the **Redcliffe Caves**. Interesting guided tours around these unusual natural caverns are conducted from time to time by the City Engineer's Department.

A stroll around Bristol city centre reveals an unusual number of interesting historic buildings. Queen Square, to the northwest of Redcliffe Bridge, is lined with handsome early 18th century buildings, although two sides had to be rebuilt following their destruction in a riot in 1831. The **Theatre Royal** in King Street is the home of the acclaimed Bristol Old Vic theatre company. One of the oldest theatres in the country still in regular use, it was built in the 1760s with a semicircular auditorium, a rare feature for the time. Also in King Street, a striking timber framed merchant's house of 1669 known as **Llandoger Trow** can be seen at its eastern end.

Continuing northwards into the area once contained within the city walls, **The Exchange** in Corn Street was built in the 1740s by the neoclassical architect, John Wood the Elder, whose work is much in evidence at Bath. The interior contains some fine detailing, including three heads symbolically depicting Asia, Africa and America which look down from above the doorways leading off the entrance hall. The four low flat-topped pillars which can be seen outside the Exchange are known as "nails". These are made of bronze and were used by local merchants to transact their business, giving rise to the saying, "to pay on the nail".

**The Red Lodge** in Park Row contains the only remaining Tudor domestic interior in Bristol. Together with a similar residence called the White Lodge, it was built for Sir John Younge in the 16th century. The building retains a remarkable number of original features, including one of the finest Tudor oak-panelled rooms in Wessex, and is now under the custodianship of the Bristol Museum and Art Gallery.

The elegant **Georgian House** in Great George Street was originally built in 1791 as a merchant's town house. Furnished in the style of the period, its contents have been selected from the permanent collection of the City Museum and Art Gallery, and include purchases made specifically for the house. The main **City Museum and Art Gallery** in Queen's Road occupies an imposing building at the top Park Street. Among its many fine exhibits is an exceptional collection of Chinese glass. Also worth seeing are **John Cabot's House** in Deanery Road and the **Trinity Almshouses** in Old Market Street to the east of the city centre.

Also to the east of town, near the Temple Meads railway station, can be found the oldest Methodist Chapel in the world, built in 1739 and known as **John Wesley's Chapel**, built by this renowned man. At the **British Empire and Commonwealth Museum** in Clock Tower Yard, exhibits trace the history of British discovery of foreign lands, and the rich cultural legacy brought about by Britain's membership in the Commonwealth.

Much of Bristol's waterfront has been now redeveloped for recreational use. **@Bristol** in Deanery Road, Harbourside is home to two unique attractions: Wildscreen, which brings visitors face to face with the natural world, and Explore, which explains the science behind the world around us and how it works. Part of a waterside redevelopment that promises to be a new cultural quarter for the city and a magnet for residents and visitors alike, it brings science, nature and art to life.

The **Bristol Industrial Museum** houses a fascinating record of the achievements of the city's industrial pioneers, including those with such household names as Harvey (wines and sherries), Fry (chocolate), Wills (tobacco) and McAdam (road building). Visitors can find out about Bristol's history as a port, view the aircraft and aero engines made in the city since 1910, and inspect some of the many famous motor vehicles which have borne the Bristol name since Victorian times. During the summer, the museum offers interesting working demonstrations of some of its more spectacular exhibits. These include a giant crane, steam railway, printing workshop and a variety of motor vessels.

An excellent museum dedicated to the pioneering Victorian engineer, Isambard Kingdom Brunel, is located in the Great Train Shed at old Temple Meads station. The nearby **Exploratory** is a hands-on educational facility designed to put fun into everyday science. Situated in Gasferry Road on the southern side of the Floating Harbour, the **Maritime Heritage Centre** is an impressive visitor attraction which is dedicated to the history of Bristol shipbuilding. Among the increasing number of historic ships which line Bristol's wharves is Brunel's mighty *SS Great Britain*, the world's first iron-hulled, propeller-driven, ocean-going vessel which was built in the city in 1843. After a working life of 43 years, it was retired to the remote Falkland Islands where it was used as a storage hulk for over 70 years until 1970, when it was saved and brought back to the dry dock of its birth.

Brunel was also responsible for designing the **Clifton Suspension Bridge**, one of Bristol's most graceful landmarks which spans the Avon gorge a mile and a half to the west of the city centre. Opened five years after his death in 1864, it continues to carry an important route into the city. The bridge is suspended more than 200 feet above the river and offers drivers and pedestrians a magnificent view over the city and surrounding landscape.

**Goldney Grotto, Bristol**

The National Trust owned **Avon Gorge Nature Reserve** on the western side of the bridge offers some delightful walking through Leigh Woods to the summit of an Iron Age hill fort. A former snuff mill on the eastern side has been converted into an observatory whose attractions include a rare working example of a camera obscura. A nearby passage leads to the Giant's Cave, a subterranean chamber which opens onto a ledge high above the Avon.

Once a genteel suburb, modern Clifton is an attractive residential area whose elegant Georgian terraces are interspersed with stylish shops and restaurants. Clifton's **Goldney House**, now a university hall, is the location of a unique subterranean folly, **Goldney Grotto**, which dates from the 1730s.

A fantastic labyrinth filled with spectacular rock formations, foaming cascades and a marble statue of Neptune, its walls are covered with thousands of seashells and "Bristol diamonds", fragments of a rare quartz found in nearby Avon Gorge. The grotto is currently undergoing an ongoing programme of conservation and restoration, but is open most weekends between Easter and September. The renowned **Bristol Zoo Gardens** are located on the northwestern edge of Clifton in Clifton Down.

# AROUND BRISTOL

BITTON                                                             Map 2 ref H2
3 miles E of Bristol off the A431/A4175

The **Avon Valley Railway** runs south from Bitton Station to Barrow Hill, and north to Oldland Common, enjoying splendid views of the surrounding countryside along the way.

KEYNSHAM                                                          Map 2 ref H2
3 miles S of Bristol off the A37

On the opposite side of the city, the former industrial centre of Keynsham lies in the sheltered valley of the River Avon, midway between Bristol and Bath. Now predominantly a dormitory town which thankfully is bypassed by the main A4, the settlement's present day atmosphere belies its ancient roots. The area is known to have been populated by the Romans and indeed, the remains of two Roman villas were discovered here during excavations for a chocolate factory which have since been incorporated into an interesting small museum near the factory entrance.

In the late 12th century, an abbey was established in Keynsham on sloping ground near the River Chew. The piousness of the medieval monks, however, left much to be desired, and eventually they had to be banned from keeping sporting dogs, going out at night, employing private washer-women, and inviting female guests into the monastery. The abbey has long since disappeared, its only remaining outbuildings having been finally laid to rest beneath the bypass. However, the part 13th century parish church has survived intact. A good example of Somerset Gothic, the interior contains some impressive monuments to members of the Bridges family. Two large brass mills were established in

Keynsham during the town's 18th century industrial heyday, one on the Avon and the other on the Chew. The former ceased production in the 1890s, and the latter in 1927, leaving behind some impressive industrial remains.

**The Brassmill** is a distinguished and distinctive public house and restaurant just on the outskirts of Keynsham. As its name suggests, it is set on the site of an old brass mill, situated near the water so that barges could easily transport the brass, imported from Holland, up and down the River Avon to be milled on this site. Popular with locals and visitors alike, this pub has a tasteful and attractive interior boasting an open-plan design, with spacious bar and dining areas. There are several different menus, including a children's menu and special dessert menu, highlighting the many delectable treats in store for diners. Everything from hearty sandwiches, baguettes and salads to delicious main beef, fish, chicken and vegetarian courses such as "surf and turf", steak and kidney pie, roasted vegetable pasta and spicy beef chilli can be found here. Both traditional favourites and innovative alternatives are on offer, as well as changing daily specials. A good range of real ales are available, together with a great wine list and fine selection of lagers, spirits and soft drinks. The pub also hosts children's parties and other functions; it is well suited for these occasions, with ample room throughout and plenty of parking space. Manager Jeanette Dyer and her friendly, helpful staff make every effort to ensure that their guests enjoy a relaxed and pleasant time. As part of the Brewers Fayre range of pubs, there's a wealth of experience and a tradition of quality service and value behind this successful and welcoming pub/restaurant. Handy for Bristol, Bath and the surrounding region, this superior pub makes an ideal retreat for a quiet drink in good company.

**The Brassmill, Avonmill Lane, Keynsham,
nr Bristol, Somerset BS31 2UG
Tel: 0117 986 7280 Fax: 0117 986 0562**

SALTFORD Map 2 ref H2

4 miles SE of Bristol off the B3116/A4175

At **Saltford Marina**, luxury narrow boats can be hired for trips along the River Avon.

**The Jolly Sailor** is a characterful and eye-catching public house set along the banks of the River Avon, adjacent to the Saltford Lock, with an attractive marina nearby. On the edge of Keynsham town centre, just a few miles from Bath and Bristol, this handsome pub has been refurbished extensively in recent years, but has re-
tained its traditional atmosphere. A raised patio garden area to the front commands a view of the river. Inside the bar has an open-plan layout, with open fires when the weather is raw. The holes burned in the man-telpiece mark a bit of local history: in days gone by, bargemen promoted to the captaincy would use a red hot poker to burn a hole here, to commemorate their promotion. Then they would be ex-pected to buy a

The Jolly Sailor, Mead Lane, Saltford,
Somerset BS31 3ER Tel: 01225 873002

round for all their pals! The light and airy Conservatory Restaurant overlooks the river. Everything from sandwiches and light snacks to full meals is available, with a range of home cooked favourites to choose from. Owners Roger and Trish Baker are friendly hosts, bringing a wealth of experience to looking after their customers and offering a professional and personable service to all.

## PENSFORD                                                   MAP 2 REF H3
6 miles S of Bristol off the A37

**Blackmore and Langdon** is a nursery specialising in breeding delphiniums and begonias. This old established family firm was started in 1901 by two friends, James Blackmore and Charles Langdon, with a mutual love of double begonias. Delphiniums were added to their lists in 1902; these two plants have remained the mainstay of the business for the past 98 years. The firm won its first Royal Horticultural Society Gold Medal in 1903. Over the years other plants were added to their superb repertoire, so that today's catalogue includes polyanthus,

phlox and aquilegia. Each year new begonias are bred and named; these are usually on display in the nursery throughout the summer months. Every year the catalogue features interesting new cultivars. The firm exhibits its beautiful plants annually at the Chelsea Flower Show and at other distinguished shows throughout the UK. The nursery is open daily, from 9-5 Mondays-Fridays; 10-4 on Saturdays and Sundays.

**Blackmore and Langdon, Stanton Nurseries, Pensford, Bristol, Somerset BS39 4JL Tel: 01275 332300 Fax: 01275 331207**

## CHEW MAGNA

MAP 2 REF G3

7 miles S of Bristol off the B3130/A37

The former wool village of Chew Magna lies on the northern side of the **Chew Valley Lake.** This pleasant community contains some handsome Georgian houses, most of which are now owned by well to do Bristol commuters. The nucleus of the village is a three sided green whose surrounding shops and pubs are linked by an unusual raised stone pavement. The striking early 16th century **Church House** at the top of the green was originally intended as a venue for holding the annual **Church Ales** and for brewing the ale and baking the bread to be sold and consumed on such occasions. Funds raised would then be used to maintain the fabric of the parish church throughout the forthcoming year. Such church houses, mostly built in the 15th or earlier 16th centuries, were mainly limited to the counties of Somerset and Devon.

Beyond it, the impressive parish **Church of St Andrew** stands as a testimony to Chew Magna's former wool-based prosperity. The interior contains a number of remarkable monuments, the most exceptional of which is the reclining wooden effigy of a knight, probably Sir John Hauteville, which shows him leaning on one elbow and resting his foot on a somewhat perplexed looking lion. There is also an interesting double effigy of Sir John Loe, a 15th century local squire who was reputed to be 7 foot tall, and his wife, and another of the Elizabethan sergeant-at-arms, Edward Baber and his wife, both of whom are sporting unusual double ruffs. Chew Court, a former summer palace of the bishops of Bath and Wells, lies behind a high wall adjacent to the churchyard.

**The Pelican Inn** in Chew Magna is a 300 year old coaching inn that is said to be one of the oldest buildings in the town. Located in the centre of town, Chew Mendip and the Chew Lakes are just a short walk away. Popular with families, locals, walkers, birdwatchers and other visitors alike, it is run by tenants Terry and Carron Priddis, who are amiable and welcoming hosts. The interior of this attractive and welcoming inn has two main bar areas. A wealth of porcelain and copper ornaments, together with old prints and photographs, adorn the walls. There's a roaring open fire on chilly days, and a separate function room.

The extensive walled garden to the rear boasts a totally secure children's play garden and, in summer, a barbecue

**The Pelican Inn, South Parade, Chew Magna, Somerset BS40 8ND Tel: 01275 332448**

area. There's a varied range of beers, wines and spirits, as well as good value for money pub food, from sandwiches to pies, curries, chicken and pasta dishes. Throughout the week there's entertainment on offer, with karaoke, live music, and charity events organised from and through the pub.

## STANTON DREW                                                MAP 2 REF G3
7 miles S of Bristol off the B3130/A37

The ancient settlement of Stanton Drew lies to the south of the B3130, a mile and a half east of Chew Magna. A prehistoric site of some importance, the village stands beside a series of stone circles over half a mile across which were constructed by the Bronze Age Beaker People between 2000 and 1600 BC. The complex of standing stones consists of three stone circles, a lone stone known as **Hauteville's Quoit**, and a large chambered burial tomb known as **The Cove**. The stones are composed of three different rock types - limestone, sandstone and conglomerate - and are thought to have been erected for religious, or perhaps astronomical, purposes. In common with many stone circles in the west of Britain, the origin of those at Stanton Drew are steeped in legend. The most widespread account tells of a foolhardy wedding party who wanted to continue dancing into the Sabbath.  At midnight, the piper refused to carry on, prompting the infuriated bride to declare that if she had to, she'd get a piper from hell. At that point, another piper stepped forward to volunteer his services and the party resumed.  But then the music began to get louder and louder and the tempo faster and faster, until the dancers were gripped in a furious jig they were powerless to stop.  They realised too late that the good natured piper was the Devil himself, and when his playing reached its terrifying climax, he turned them all to stone. To this day, this curious group of standing stones continues to be known as "The Wedding".

The village of Stanton Drew also contains a number of noteworthy old buildings, many of which are listed.  Among them is the 15th century stone bridge over the River Chew, an unusual hexagonal thatched dwelling which later served as a turnpike tollhouse, and an assortment of handsome 17th and 18th century private residences.

A couple of miles to the north of Stanton Drew, the line of the ancient **Wansdyke** runs in a roughly east-west direction around the southern edge of Bristol.  This great earthwork bank was built during the Dark Ages as a boundary line and defensive barrier against the Saxons.  Although most evidence of its existence has long since disappeared, short sections can still be identified, for example along the ridge adjoining the Iron Age hill fort on Stantonbury Hill, east of Compton Dando, and at Maes Knoll, four miles further west.

Set amid mature gardens and situated at the end of a quiet lane, **Valley Farm** is a large and handsome stonebuilt farmhouse offering bed and breakfast accommodation. This warm and welcoming family home is furnished and decorated to a high standard of taste, comfort and quality. The River Chew runs

**Valley Farm, Sandy Lane, Stanton Drew, nr Bristol, Somerset  BS39 4EL**
**Tel/Fax: 01275 332723**

nearby. Near to Bath, Bristol, Cheddar and Wells, this makes a perfect base from which to explore the region. There are three superb double guest bedrooms, two en suite and one with private bath. The guests' lounge is also beautifully furnished, and has a number of diversions (television, radio, books and tourism brochures). Breakfast - whether the full English or a vegetarian alternative - is hearty and delicious. The Chew Valley Lakes are renowned for their trout fishing, while there are many fine walks in the area. Owner Doreen Keel is a friendly and welcoming host, who is happy to provide her guests with information about the area.

## CHEW STOKE                                                   MAP 2 REF G3
8 miles S of Bristol off the B3131/A37

Close to the Chew Valley lake, which is excellent for fly fishing and bird watching, **The Stoke Inn** is a traditional country inn built some 300 years ago. The impressive stonebuilt exterior offers visitors a hint of what's inside: a cosy, comfortable and traditional Somerset pub with a warm welcome and open log fires.

The Stoke Inn has a traditional public bar with pub games; darts, table skittles and shove ha'penny. It also offers a cosy lounge and has an excellent restaurant situated in the old stables where superb home-cooked dishes are served and prepared by the chef. Please note the restaurant is non-smoking.

**Stoke Inn, Bristol Road, Chew Stoke, Somerset BS40 8XE Tel/Fax: 01275 332120**

The inn offers a full range of real ales, ciders and soft drinks. It is open all day Saturdays, Sundays and Bank Holidays. In addition to the bar and restaurant the Bilbie Room offers facilities for functions up to 100 people.

## CLUTTON HILL
MAP 2 REF H3

9 miles S of Bristol off the A37/A368

Well worth seeking out is **The Hunters Rest** in Clutton Hill. Voted Family Pub of the Year by the Bristol Evening Post, this superb establishment occupies a secluded, elevated position with delightful views across the Cam Valley. Handy for Bristol, Bath, Wells and many other attractions in the area, and within sight of the Mendip Hills, this charming pub has a welcoming atmosphere enhanced by the friendly and personable owner Paul Thomas and his staff. Built of locally

**The Hunters Rest, King Lane, Clutton Hill, Bristol, Somerset BS39 5QL**
**Tel: 01761 452303 Fax: 01761 453308**

quarried stone in the 1800s as a hunting lodge for the Earl of Warwick's estate, it was sold at the beginning of the 20th century and became a tavern, originally serving the mining community. The open-plan interior has plenty of comfortable seating and is furnished to a high standard of taste and quality. The ceiling and wall timbers are adorned with ceramics, copper and brass implements, old muskets and sabres. A scale model of a King George V steam locomotive is on display in the public bar area. The food available is delicious and cooked to order. The extensive menu boasts a changing selection of both traditional and more innovative dishes, including tempting morsels such as Stilton and broccoli pie, fillet steak, lamb balti and smoked haddock, along with a range of rolls and sandwiches made with freshly baked bread, and many other mouth-watering options. There's a wide range of real ales on tap, as well as a good choice of beers, wines and spirits. The lovely beer garden boasts the added attraction of a wonderful miniature railway, attracting enthusiasts and families in fine weather. One-third of a mile long, it carries passengers through the landscaped gardens every weekend in summer (weather permitting). Accommodation will also be available at this excellent location during the lifetime of this book. Please telephone for details.

## BARROW GURNEY
MAP 2 REF G2

4 miles SW of Bristol off the A38

Prior to the building of the Blagdon and Chew Valley lakes, Bristol's fresh water came from the three small reservoirs at Barrow Gurney, a mile and a half to the west of Dundry. The first of these opened in 1852, but within two years it developed a leak and had to be drained, causing serious disruption to the city's water supply. The villages to the southwest of Bristol have undergone considerable change since the Second World War, many having now become little more than dormitory settlements for the city's commuters.

## BURRINGTON
MAP 2 REF G3

9 miles SW of Bristol off the A38

At the foot of the Mendips, handy for Bristol, Cheddar, Wells and all the other sights and attractions of this part of Somerset, **The Plume of Feathers** is a distinguished and welcoming inn and restaurant. Built some 300 years ago of local stone, there is an extensive lawned garden to the rear with secure children's play area and apple orchard. The inn sits alongside the pretty stream which runs through this picturesque village. Owners Paul and Clare are energetic and youthful hosts who take great pains to see that all their guests have an enjoyable and relaxing meal or stay. The interior boasts beamed ceilings, open fires, old settles and artwork by local artists and old photographs adorning the walls. The menu offers a range of hearty and satisfying traditional beef, pork and vegetarian dishes; there is also a good range of sandwiches and light meals. Everything is home-cooked and home-prepared. Cream teas can also be taken, either indoors or, when the weather is fine, in the lovely garden area. The ac-

**The Plume of Feathers, Rickford, nr Burrington, Somerset BS40 7AH
Tel: 01761 462682**

commodation comprises four superb and recently refurbished bedrooms which offer a high standard of luxury and comfort.

## CONGRESBURY
MAP 2 REF F3

9 miles SW of Bristol on the A370

Congresbury is a sizable village which stands at the junction of the A370 and B3133, 6 miles to the southwest of Barrow Gurney, and could be seen as just another commuter town. However, its present-day character belies a long and eventful history which goes back to the days of the Romans. At that time, the settlement stood at the end of a spur of the Somerset marshes, and fragments of Roman and pre-Saxon pottery have been found on the site of the ancient hill fort which overlooks the present village.

The early Celtic missionary, St Congar, is believed to have founded an early wattle chapel at Congresbury in the 6th century. A tree bound by an iron hoop on the eastern side of the present day church is still referred to as, **"St Congar's Walking Stick"**. This is reputed to have grown from the saint's staff which miraculously sprouted leaves after he had thrust it into the ground outside the chapel.

Congresbury's present church is a spacious, part 13th century structure with a soaring spire and a handsome Norman font which demonstrates some fine cable-carving. The striking ecclesiastical-looking building which can be glimpsed through the trees from the churchyard is the part 15th century vicarage. This was extended during the Regency period to create a curious architectural hybrid. Its distinct period styles now appear side by side, the medieval part serving as the church function room and the newer wing as the vicarage.

## PUXTON
MAP 2 REF F3

10 miles SW of Bristol off the A370

The peaceful community of Puxton lies down a lane to the south of the A370 Weston-super-Mare road, two miles to the west of Congresbury. The village is worth a look for its eccentric church tower, which leans over at such an angle it looks as if it might topple at any minute, causing its precarious looking weathercock to nose dive into the churchyard. The church interior appears to have little changed since the main body of the building was rebuilt in the 1530s, a wonderful collection of high box pews, old wooden benches and later Jacobean fittings which include the pulpit, reading desk and altar rails.

## BANWELL
MAP 2 REF F3

14 miles SW of Bristol on the A368

A narrow lane to the south of Puxton leads to Banwell, a pleasant settlement which once boasted a Saxon monastery. The village church has an impressive tower with a single turret and a striking interior with a fine rood screen and a

Norman stone font. The latter is covered in unusual carvings and is topped by a curious pointed cover, both of which belong to later eras. The village also contains a substantial Victorian mansion known as **Banwell Castle**.

In 1821, a remarkable series of caverns was discovered on Banwell Hill, above and to the west of the village. Known as the **Bone Caves**, they were found to discover the remains of prehistoric mammals, including bison, bear and reindeer. Some years later, the local bishop created an extravagant romantic park around the entrance to the caves which he filled with pyramids, monk's cells, fairy cottages and other fanciful buildings. The Avon Ski Centre and Mendip Riding Centre are two first-rate facilities which are located on the same site between the villages of Sandford and Churchill, a couple of miles to the east of Banwell.

The A371 to the west of Banwell skirts around the northern edge of the Bleadon Hills as it heads towards Weston-super-Mare on the Bristol Channel coast. A couple of miles after crossing the M5, the road passes Weston Airport, home of the world's largest collection of helicopters and autogyros. The only museum in Britain dedicated to rotary wing aircraft, the **International Helicopter Museum** is a friendly volunteer-run establishment which has over forty exhibits ranging from single-seater autogyros to giant multi-seater helicopters. There are also displays on the history and development of these remarkable flying machines, a flight simulator, and a conservation hangar where aircraft are restored.

## WESTON-SUPER-MARE Map 2 ref E3
12 miles SW of Bristol on the A370

Weston-super-Mare is of course a popular seaside resort; in recent years it has also developed as a centre of light industry. In 1811, the town was still just a fishing hamlet, with only 170 inhabitants; however, within the next 100 years it had grown to become the second largest town in Somerset. It now boasts a population of well over 50,000. Despite its relatively modern character, the locality has been inhabited since prehistoric times. The wooded promontory at the northern end of Weston Bay was the site of a sizable Iron Age hill settlement known as **Worlebury Camp**. In the 1st century AD, this was reputedly attacked and captured by the ancient Romans with great loss of life, an event confirmed by recent excavations which revealed a number of skeletons showing the effects of sword damage. A pleasant walk from the town now leads up through attractive woodland to the ancient hilltop site from where there is a magnificent view across the mouth of the Severn to Wales. Another spectacular view can be had from the clifftop site of the semi-ruined church at Uphill, a part-Norman structure which is situated at the southern end of Weston Bay, a couple of miles to the south. Weston-super-Mare has little of the grandiose architecture which characterises earlier seaside resorts such as Brighton or Torquay. Instead, it developed on a more comfortable scale with plenty of wide boulevards, leafy parks and open spaces. The town's greatest resource is its long safe sandy beach which is ideal for paddling, sunbathing and ball games. However, its gentle incline means that swimmers have to wade out a long way to find water deep enough to take the plunge.

Weston's early tourist development took place in the 1830s around the Knightstone, an islet joined to the shore at the northern end of Weston Bay onto which was eventually built a large theatre and swimming baths. Following the arrival of the railway in 1841, the town began its most rapid period of development and in 1867, a pier was built on the headland below Worlebury Camp which connected offshore Birnbeck Island with the mainland. Intended mainly as a berth for steamer traffic, it was found to be slightly off the tourist track and in due course, a more impressive pier was built nearer the town centre which, prior to serious fires in the 1930s and during the Second World War, was approximately twice its present length. Now, as then, the **Grand Pier** stands at the centre of an area crammed with souvenir shops, ice cream parlours, cafes and assorted attractions which are designed to appeal to the holidaymaker. Weston's indoor attractions include the **Winter Gardens** on the seafront, and the fascinating **Time Machine Museum** in Burlington Street.

**Woodspring Museum
Weston-super-Mare**

The Museum Trail sponsored by the **Woodspring Museum**, also in Burlington Street, begins at the Tourist Information Centre on the seafront and offers visitors to take part in a "treasure hunt" for carved stones created by artist Michael Fairfax, which lead to the Museum itself. The fine **Sea Life Aquarium** features over 30 fascinating displays and offers a full programme of feeding demonstrations, talks and special presentations. The **Weston Miniature Railway** leads from Marine Parade over half a mile around an 18 hole putting course and along the Beach Lawns overlooking the seafront.

The narrow coast road to the north of Weston-Super-Mare passes along the beach at Sand Bay before terminating at Middle Hope, a high ridge jutting out into the Severn Channel whose western end, **Sand Point**, provides another fine viewpoint. The ridge overlooks a lonely salt marsh which is home to a wide variety of wading birds, including shelduck and oystercatchers. To the east, a path leads down to the Landmark Trust-owned **Woodspring Priory**, a surprisingly intact medieval monastery which was founded around 1220 by a grandson of one of Thomas à Becket's murderers, William de Courtenay. The priory fell into disrepair following the surrender by the last prior in 1536 and its buildings were given over to agricultural use for many years. However, the church, tower, refectory and tithe barn have all survived, and the outline of the cloister can also be made out.

## CLEVEDON                                              MAP 2 REF F2
8 miles W of Bristol on the B3130

The impressive National Trust-owned **Clevedon Court** lies near junction 20 on the M5, five miles northeast of Woodspring Priory. One of the earliest surviving country houses in Britain, the main part dates from the early 14th century, and the tower and great hall are even older, dating from the 12th and 13th centuries respectively. Once partly fortified, this imposing manor house has been the home of the Elton family since 1709. Longstanding patrons of the arts, during the early 19th century they invited some of the finest poets and writers of their day to Clevedon Court, including Coleridge, Thackeray and Tennyson.

A few decades later, another member of the family invented a special technique for making the type of brightly coloured pottery which became known as Eltonware. Particularly popular in the United States, many fine examples are now on display at the house, along with a collection of rare glass from the works at Nailsea.

Clevedon Court is set within a delightful terraced garden which is known for its rare plants and shrubs. An attractive footpath leads up from here through nearby Clevedon Court Woods onto a ridge overlooking the Gordano valley. Clevedon Court is situated

**Clevedon Court, Clevcedon**

on the eastern edge of Clevedon, a genteel seaside town on the Severn estuary which has a population of around 20,000. A stylish holiday resort and residential centre since the late 18th century, at one time it was larger and more popular than Weston-super-Mare. Its seafront is lined with bright stucco-fronted Regency and mid-Victorian houses in marked contrast to the grey limestone and brick of those further inland.

Although the town contains few of the popular attractions one would normally associate with a holiday resort, the exception is **Clevedon Pier**, a remarkably slim and elegant structure which was built in the 1860s from iron rails which were intended for Brunel's ill-considered South Wales railway. When part of the pier collapsed in the 1970s, its long-term future was placed in jeopardy. During the 1980s, however, a major programme of restoration was begun which took around ten years to complete. Throughout the summer the pier is used as a landing stage by large pleasure steamers such as the *Balmoral* and the *Waverley*, the only surviving seagoing paddle steamers in the world.

Among Clevedon's many fine old buildings is the **Market Hall** of 1869 which was built to provide a place for local market gardeners to sell their produce. The largely Norman parish church of St Andrew contains some poignant memorials to local parishioners, many of whom died young. The Poet's Walk, a flower-lined footpath said to be popular with Victorian bards, begins at Clevedon promenade and leads up around Church and Wain's hills. The latter is topped by the remains of an Iron Age coastal fort and offers some magnificent views over the Severn estuary, the Levels, and the town itself. Clevedon's appeal continues to be romantic rather than dramatic. Its geographical position and lack of railway access prevented the large-scale development which so transformed other seaside resorts, and as a consequence it has managed to retain an atmosphere of tranquil refinement which still has a certain charm.

The **No 5 Coffee Shop and Bistro** in Clevedon is set opposite the beach and next to the pier, within five minutes of the town centre. From here, superb views of the Bristol Channel accompany the excellent range of dishes to enjoy. This quintessential English tea room/licensed restaurant is decorated and fur-

**No 5 Coffee Shop & Bistro, The Beach, Clevedon, Somerset BS21 7QU Tel: 01275 341633**

nished with style and taste. Handsome photographs and prints adorn the walls, which are painted in tasteful pastel shades. All dishes are freshly prepared and cooked on the premises by the qualified full-time chefs. The service is friendly and attentive, and fresh ingredients are the hallmark of all the snacks, light bites and meals on the menu. There's an extensive range of delicious savouries, sandwiches, light meals, salads and home-made cakes on offer, complemented by a good selection of speciality teas and coffees, soft drinks, lagers or spirits and a superb wine list. Here in relaxed and comfortable surroundings, guests are sure to enjoy the mouth-watering dishes available. On fine days meals are served on the sunny patio. Open: seven days a week 9.30-5; also Wednesday - Saturday 7-late.

## WALTON-IN-GORDANO                                     MAP 2 REF F2
8 miles W of Bristol on the B3124

To the northeast of Clevedon, two sweeping ridges of hills diverge like a great V. Between them lies the low Gordano valley, an area of former marshland dotted with settlements which incorporate the valley's name. Among them is Walton-in-Gordano, a small village containing an exceptionally beautiful four-acre garden, the **Manor House**, which is planted with rare shrubs, trees and herbaceous plants. To the southeast, the land rises sharply towards **Cadbury Camp**, an Iron Age hill fort situated in a dramatic position between the M5 and the village of Tickenham from where there is a fine view over the Levels to the Mendip hills.

## PORTISHEAD                                            MAP 2 REF F2
5 miles W of Bristol on the A369

The old coastal town of Portishead lies on the Severn estuary, four miles to the northeast of Clevedon. A resort whose early development had much in common with its near neighbour to the southwest, its customary villas, hotels, pier and bath houses (or saltings) began appearing in the 1820s and 1830s. The town's character changed abruptly in 1867, however, when the railway arrived to transform it into a busy port and industrial centre. A number of seaside attractions nevertheless remained, although these were largely redirected towards the cheaper end of the market. Today, Portishead is a flourishing residential centre whose finest features are its part 14th-century parish church, the Court, a handsome Tudor residence with an unusual polygonal tower, and **Portishead Point**, an impressive wooded viewpoint overlooking the Severn estuary.

The area to the northeast of Portishead around the mouth of the Bristol Avon is one which generally should be avoided by the casual visitor. Substantial modern dock facilities have been constructed on either side of the river to handle today's ocean-going cargo ships which are too gigantic to make it through the narrow Avon gorge to Bristol. Avonmouth, on the northern bank, is a place of heavy industrial activity which may inspire a certain awe when viewed from the M5 Avon Bridge.

## HENBURY

Map 2 ref G1

4 miles NW of Bristol on the A4018

A couple of noteworthy places of interest can be found on the northwestern approaches to Bristol. The modern suburb of Henbury contains the remarkable

**Blaise Hamlet**

Georgian oasis of **Blaise Hamlet**, a collection of nine detached stone cottages which were designed in romantic rustic style by John Nash in 1809. Each was built to a different design for the retired estate workers of the nearby Blaise Estate. The cottages themselves are not open to the public, although visitors enjoy free access to the village green. An interesting museum of everyday life is housed in nearby **Blaise Castle House**, a late 18th-century mansion set within 400 acres of parkland which once formed the nucleus of the estate. Displays include toys, costumes and household equipment.

## WESTBURY ON TRYM

Map 2 ref G2

2 miles NW of Bristol on the A38

Nearby Westbury-on-Trym is the location of the National Trust-owned **Westbury College Gatehouse**, the 15th century gatehouse of a now-demolished ecclesiastical college. (Open by arrangement with the local vicar.)

# 3 The Eastern Mendips

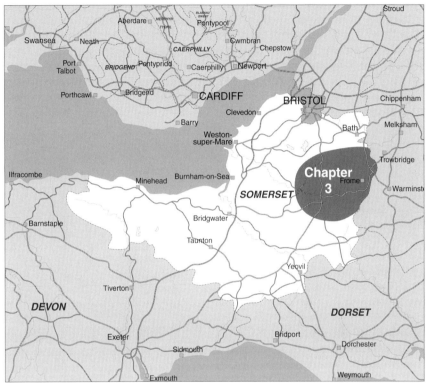

© MAPS IN MINUTES ™ (1998)

## FROME

Standing beside the river from which it takes its name, the ancient settlement of Frome is the largest centre of population in northeast Somerset, and the fourth largest town in the county. The parish **Church of St John the Baptist** was founded as a Saxon monastic house by St Aldhelm, Abbot of Malmesbury, in the 7th century. By the time of the Norman invasion, Frome was already a sizeable market town which extended from the river to the church on the hill above.

The **Frome valley** became an important centre of the wool industry during the late Middle Ages when a series of weirs was constructed to regulate the flow of water to the many water-powered weaving and fulling mills which lined the riverbank. (Fulling was a process which softened and increased the volume of woven cloth by immersing it in water and feeding it through a series of mechanically-driven rollers.) However, the industry largely collapsed in the 18th century when textile production transferred to the industrial North, although one mill, A H Tucker's, continued in production right up until the 1960s.

The prolonged decline of the textile industry meant that little of central Frome was redeveloped during the 19th and early 20th centuries, and as a result, many of its narrow medieval streets and alleyways have survived intact. Some have wonderful names like Pudding Bag Lane and Twattle Alley, and others, such as Gentle Street, the steeply-sloping Catherine Hill, and Cheap Street with its water course running down the centre, are highly impressive in their own right. The bridge over the River Frome incorporates an 18th century lockup gaol, near to which can be seen the famous Bluecoat School and the restored **Blue House**, an elegant almshouse dating from 1726.

Best explored on foot, the centre of Frome is an attractive conservation area which contains an unusual number of interesting shops, cafes and residential buildings. Lively markets continue to be held in the town every day but Tuesday and Sunday, and for those interested in local history, the excellent **Frome Museum** is open Wednesday to Saturday (it is advised you ring first to check times: 01373 467271). There is also an interesting arts complex, the **Black Swan Guild**, situated in Bridge Street, with workshops, gallery, craft shop and restaurant. .

**Quintessence** is the delightful name of a truly unique showcase for top-quality artists and craftspeople. Not far from the town centre along a cobbled street in the older and historic part of Frome, this fine shop occupies a traditional 200-year-old building. Brimming with a kaleidoscope of colours, textures, designs and styles, this wonderful shop is a celebration of contemporary arts and crafts. Much

**Quintessence, 21 Paul Street, Catherine Hill, Frome, Somerset BA11 1DT  Tel/Fax: 01373 461352**

of the work on sale was created by local artists and craftspeople, and includes carvings, knitwear, woven rugs and throws, hand-thrown pottery, paintings, drawings, blown glass objects and many other treasures. Giftware of the highest quality is the order the day here. Specialist exhibitions are held throughout the year, highlighting a particular theme (such as sculpture or hand-spun fabrics). Work in a variety of media is always available, some of it traditional, some more innovative. Whether searching for something special for the home or for an individual or unusual gift, look no further.

## AROUND FROME

OLDFORD                                          MAP 3 REF I4
2 miles NE of Frome off the A36

At the edge of Frome along the Bath Road, adjacent to Longleat House and many other local attractions, **The Ship at Oldford** is a spacious and traditional brickbuilt public house dating back some 150 years. Set amid an eighth of an acre, there's a large and handsome beer/tea garden to the rear enclosed and secure for children - the perfect place to relax with a drink or some of the great home-made food. All dishes - from snacks and sandwiches to the excellent Sunday roasts - use only the freshest local produce. The interior boasts two bar areas, open fires and a wealth of attractive details in the furnishings and

**The Ship at Oldford, Frome Road, Oldford, nr Frome, Somerset BA11 2ND Tel: 01373 462043**

decor, including many original features such as the exposed stone walls. There's an excellent range of real ales, lagers, wines and spirits on offer. Owners Richard and Jill Pullen are welcoming and friendly hosts, and the atmosphere throughout this fine pub is relaxed and welcoming.

## BECKINGTON
Map 3 ref I3
4 miles NE of Frome off the A36

To the north of Frome the river winds its way towards its confluence with the Bristol Avon. Three miles downstream, the former wool village of Beckington boasts one of the largest and most ornate Norman church towers in Somerset, with the rest of the building being predominantly 15th century Perpendicular. The village contains the some fine stonebuilt houses, including the early Georgian **Cedars**, a possible former ecclesiastical hospice for Augustinian canons known as the **Abbey**, and **Seymour's Court**. Seymour's Court takes its name from the family of St Maur. Sir John St Maur of Rode married the heiress of the Erlegh family, earlier lords of Beckington manor.

## LULLINGTON
Map 3 ref I3
4 miles NW of Frome off the A36

The peaceful community of Lullington lies on the opposite bank of the river, a mile and a half to the southwest of Beckington. The Norman village church is worth a look for its remarkable carved north doorway - a striking combination of arched lintels and twisted columns crowned by a mysterious seated figure. A gateway on the southern edge of the village marks the start of the footpath to **Orchardleigh Park**, an imposing Victorian pile which was built in the 1850s. The lake in the grounds has an island in its western corner on which is perched a small church whose churchyard contains the grave of Sir Henry Newbolt, the author of Drake's Drum, who died in 1938.

## RODE
Map 3 ref I3
5 miles NE of Frome off the A361

Situated between the A36 and A361 a mile to the north of Beckington, the pretty village of Rode is the location of the famous **Rode Bird Gardens**. This impressive 17 acre park is home to over 200 different species of exotic birds from around the world, many of which are allowed to fly freely. The grounds incorporate a miniature woodland steam railway, a pets' corner, and a series of lakes inhabited by flamingos, penguins and many other species of birds and waterfowl. There is also an ambitious captive breeding programme dedicated to the rearing of rare and endangered species.

## NORTON ST PHILIP
Map 3 ref I3
6 miles N of Frome off the A366

One of the finest medieval inns in Britain can be found in Norton St Philip, a lovely old village which lies a couple of miles to the northwest of Rode near the junction of the A366 and B3110 Bath road. Recorded in the Domesday Book of 1086, in the 13th century some land near the village was given to Carthusian monks, and the nearby Priory was completed in 1232. The monks were responsible for building the village's most famous landmark - the splendid **George Inn**. Established as a house of hospitality , nearby Hinton Priory is the second-oldest Carthusian monastery in the country.  The timber framed upper floors were added in the 15th century when the inn doubled as a warehouse for storing locally produced woollen cloth.  Rumour has it that, in 1668, the diarist Samuel Pepys stayed here with his family while on his way to Bath, recording the experience simply as, "Dined well. 10 shillings."

A decade and a half later, the ill-fated Duke of Monmouth made the George his temporary headquarters shortly before the Battle of Sedgemoor in 1685. According to local legend, twelve men implicated in the ill fated uprising were imprisoned here after the battle in what is now the Dungeon Bar.  Later they were taken away and hanged, drawn and quartered - probably in the local market place.  Virtually unaltered since, the present-day inn is a wonderful fusion of medieval stonework, oriel windows and timber framing.  There is also a superb courtyard and minstrels' gallery at the rear.

Set in the heart of the conservation village of Norton St Philip, **The Plaine** is a delightful family home dating back to the 16th century and offering excellent bed and breakfast accommodation. The house has been extensively renovated, but still retains many original features - combining the best of traditional comfort with modern convenience. All three en suite guest bedrooms boast beautiful four-poster beds and are furnished and decorated with taste and style. Comfortable yet informal, the ambience at this marvellous estab-

**The Plaine, Bell Hill, Norton St Philip, Bath, Somerset BA3 6LT Tel: 01373 834723  Fax: 01373 834101 e-mail: theplaine@easynet.co.uk website: www.theplaine.com**

lishment makes it a welcome retreat. Just 10 minutes' drive from Bath, it makes an ideal base for exploring this part of Somerset. Breakfast is served in the handsome dining room, with its exposed beam ceiling and impressive stone fireplace.

Owners Sarah and John Webster are welcoming hosts, happy to cater for special dietary requirements. The Plaine is a non-smoking establishment.

A former wool village which once stood on the main Bath to Salisbury road, Norton St Philip also contains some fine 17th century stone cottages and a handsome, mainly Perpendicular church. **St Philip's** was rebuilt in the 17th century and is believed to contain the grave of the Siamese-twin sisters who were born in the nearby hamlet of Foxcote. Their tombstone, which survives under the tower of Norton St Philip church, is reputed to have been carved with a likeness of the girls who had "two bodies upward and one stomach".

Just off the main Trowbridge-to-Bath road, **Norwood Farm** is an organic farm occupying 300 acres, which began as a rare breeds farm and then expanded to include more markets - such as beef, lamb, pigs - over recent years. Manager Marcus Bradshaw is a stalwart supporter of the aims and principles of organic farming, and this organic farm is a tribute to his dedication. The many special features of this superb farm include over 30 rare and beautiful animal breeds, including Saddleback pigs in "pigloos", Shetland ponies and Wiltshire Horn sheep, a recycling area with information on how we can all contribute to conserving the Earth's valuable resources, a wind turbine providing wind-powered electricity to the fridges and freezers in the cafe and shop, and tailor-made edu-

**Norwood Farm, Bath Road, Norton St Philip, Somerset BA3 6LP
Tel: 01373 834356 Fax: 01373 834884**

cational programmes for school groups of all ages. Guided walks around the farm are also available for groups. The safe play area for children is also wonderful. The display area is suitable for pushchairs and wheelchairs. The farm trail takes about an hour and includes six stiles. The farm encourages biodiversity not just with its rare breeds but with the woods, hedges and ponds on the farm, which provide homes for a great variety of wildlife species. The farm produces healthy, safe foods and the farm trails provide access to some beautiful countryside. In the attractive tea room, visitors can enjoy teas, coffees, cold drinks, hot and cold light meals (including many organic dishes), snacks, cakes and sandwiches. In the farm shop, everything from gifts and tea towels, T-shirts, magazines, literature about organic farming methods and souvenirs to organic meats, vegetables and cheeses is available. Open: 10.30-6 from two weeks before Easter to mid-September.

## FARLEIGH HUNGERFORD
MAP 3 REF I3
6 miles NE of Frome on the A366

The old fortified settlement of Farleigh Hungerford lies on the A366 Radstock to Trowbridge road, two miles to the northeast of Norton St Philip. The village is worth visiting for the impressive remains of **Farleigh Hungerford Castle**, a medieval fortification which stands on a rise above the River Frome to the northeast of the centre. The structure was built by Sir Thomas Hungerford, the first Speaker of the House of Commons, on the site of an old manor house which he acquired in the late 14th century. According to local lore, Sir Thomas failed to obtain proper permission from the Crown for his fortifications, an oversight which almost led to his downfall. However, the Hungerfords were a powerful family who owned land throughout Wiltshire, and so he was able to pacify the situation and survive the king's displeasure.

A century and a half later, another member of the Hungerford family was less successful in avoiding royal disfavour. After having imprisoned his wife in one of the castle towers for four years, he was eventually executed in 1540 by Henry VIII for "treason and unnatural vice". The castle then changed hands in the early 18th century; however, the new owners saw the structure more as a stone quarry than a place to live and proceeded to remove most of its walls to build a new Gothic-style mansion on the opposite side of the village. Nevertheless, an impressive shell of towers and perimeter walls has survived intact, along with the castle **Chapel of St Leonard's**. This contains a striking 15th century mural of St George, some fine stained glass and a number of interesting monuments, including the tomb of Sir Thomas Hungerford himself. Farleigh Hungerford Castle was brought under the ownership of English Heritage early in the 20th century.

## NUNNEY
MAP 3 REF I4
3 miles SW of Frome off the A361

Another fortification with an interesting history can be found at Nunney, a picturesque community which lies in the lanes to the north of the A361 Shepton Mallet road, three miles to the southwest of Frome. The focus of this small former market town is its dramatic moated **Castle** which was begun in 1373 by Sir John de la Mare on his return from the French wars. Thought to be modelled on the Bastille, the structure consists of four solidly built towers which stand on an island formed by a stream on one side and a broad water filled moat on the other. The castle came under Parliamentarian artillery fire during the English Civil War and, despite having a garrison of only one officer, eight men and a handful of civilian refugees, held out for two days. The bombardment, however, damaged the building beyond repair and it had to be abandoned, leaving the romantic remains which can be seen today.

One of the 30-pound cannonballs which helped to demolish the castle walls is on view in Nunney's 13th century **All Saints' Church**. Reached via a footbridge over the moat and another over a small stream, this much altered building also contains an interesting model of the castle in its original condition, as well as a number of tombs to the de la Mare family, including an impressive stone effigy of Sir Philip. Nunney's old **Market Place**, which was granted a trading licence by the Crown in 1260, is also worth a visit.

## WHATLEY
Map 3 ref H4
3 miles W of Frome off the A361/A362

A mile to the north of Nunney, the road to Mells passes through the attractive village of Whatley, the location of an interesting vineyard and herb garden.

Adjacent to Whatley's church of St George, **Whatley Vineyard and Herb Garden** has two acres of vines and a quarter-acre of herbs. Four grape varieties are grown here: Seyval Blanc, Huxelrebe, Schonburger, and Madeleine Angevine. All these varieties have been chosen for their suitability to the local soils and climate. Visitors are given the opportunity to wander through the vineyard and enjoy the secluded beauty of the walled herb garden. The herb garden is laid out in the shape of a cross, as was traditional in monastic herb gardens of the Middle Ages to ward off evil spirits. Enclosed by a high wall, the garden is protected from harsh winds and offers a peaceful and scented retreat. The farm shop in the grounds offers a superb range of herbs, wines, ciders and jams, all locally produced. Group tours and winetastings can be

**Whatley Vineyard and Herb Garden, The Old Rectory, Whatley, Frome, Somerset BA11 3LA**
**Tel/Fax: 01373 836467**

arranged, taking in the herb garden, vineyard and the cellars, followed by a light meal.

GREAT ELM MAP 3 REF I4
2½ miles NW of Frome off the A362

**Church House** is a warm and comfortable rural retreat set in the heart of the peaceful hamlet of Great Elm, near Frome. This traditional stonebuilt home, adjacent to the Norman church of St Mary Magdalen, dates back to the 1500s. The surrounding area is a veritable haven of tranquillity and beauty, abounding in wildlife and with the rushing Mells Water within 300 yards of the house. There are a number of interesting long-distance walks that start from the door-

step, as the East Mendip Way, Wyvern Way and MacMillan Way all pass within 100 yards of the house. Here at this charming home from home, all the warmth and cosiness of a quintessentially English dwelling await the visitor. Breakfast comes with all the trimmings; several nearby pubs offer

**Church House, Great Elm, Frome, Somerset  BA11 3NZ**
**Tel: 01373 813215**

good evening meals. Owner Judy Duffus is a welcoming and conscientious host. Some of her guests arrive from the nearby Jackdaws Educational Trust, a distinguished centre for classical music courses held throughout the year. Guests at Church House are welcome to combine a visit here with a weekend course at Jackdaws, or a visit to enjoy one of the concerts given there (for more information and booking, please telephone 01373 812383).

**Jackdaws Educational Trust** is a centre for musical excellence founded in 1993 by former international mezzo-soprano and current Artistic Director Maureen Lehane with the support of Jackdaws Patron Dame Joan Sutherland. The Trust grew out of the successful Great Elm Music Festival (1987-98). Its mission is to provide an opportunity for people to discover that the deepest pleasure in and appreciation for music comes from understanding and hard work. Set in a converted stable block by a millpond in the picturesque Vallis

Vale, Jackdaws holds an all year round programme of weekend courses and workshops for amateur musicians and young professionals on piano music, chamber music, Italian opera and many other disciplines. There is also a distinguished concert series of top-class

**Jackdaws Educational Trust, Bridge House, Great Elm, Frome, Somerset BA11 3NY Tel: 01373 812383 Fax: 01373 812083 e-mail: music@jackdaws.org website: www.jackdaws.org**

classical music performances. These superb concerts, and the residential music courses, benefit from the tranquillity and beauty of Jackdaws' rural setting and a superior standard of musical instruction and accomplishment.

## MELLS                                                                    MAP 3 REF H4
3 miles NW of Frome off the A362

Mells must be one of the loveliest villages in northeast Somerset. Once the easternmost limit of the lands belonging to the mighty Glastonbury Abbey, Abbot Selwood drew up plans to rebuild the village in the shape of a St Anthony's cross (a cross with four arms of equal length) in the 15th century. Only one, **New Street**, was completed; this architectural gem can be seen to the south of St Andrew's parish church. The church itself is a magnificent example of Somerset Perpendicular, with a soaring 104 foot tower and spectacular pinnacled south porch. The interior contains a remarkable collection of monuments designed by some of the 20th century's most acclaimed artists, including Lutyens, Gill, Munnings and Burne-Jones. One is to Raymond Asquith, the eldest son of the Liberal Prime Minister, Herbert Asquith, who was killed during the First World War. A memorial to the pacifist and antiwar poet Siegfried Sassoon can be seen in the churchyard.

According to legend, the Abbot of Glastonbury, in an attempt to stave off Henry VIII's Dissolution of the Monasteries, dispatched his steward, John Horner, to London with a gift for the King consisting of a pie into which was baked the title deeds of 12 ecclesiastical manor houses. Far from persuading Henry, however, Horner returned to Somerset the rightful owner of three of the manors himself - Mells, Nunney and Leigh-upon-Mendip - for which he paid of total of £2000. This remarkable act of disloyalty is supposedly commemorated in the nursery rhyme Little Jack Horner which describes how Jack "put in his thumb and pulled out a plum", i.e. the deeds to the property. The manor house at Mells, which is not open to the public, remained in the hands of the Horner family until the early 20th century when it passed to the Asquiths by marriage.

Hidden in the lanes to the northwest of Mells, the 18th century country mansion **Babington House** stands at the end of a striking avenue of beech trees, a mile from the A362 Frome to Radstock road. Dating from around 1700, with a wing of 1790, the house and nearby church of St Margaret form an elegant composition. The church, with its original timber panelling and box pews, is a rarity in Somerset having been left virtually unchanged since it was constructed in 1750. These two buildings are the only evidence of the medieval hamlet of Babington, a settlement which suffered as a result the 18th century fashion for emparking - that is, removing the dwellings of the local inhabitants in order to create an uninterrupted view of the landscaped grounds from the big house.

## COLEFORD
MAP 3 REF H4
4 miles W of Frome off the A361

Set in a picturesque valley with a long and proud history in mining and farming, **The Kings Head** in Coleford is a traditional public house with a welcoming feel. Owners Robin and Shirley Thompson have run this fine pub for some 30 years. Robin, and ex-miner, was born in the village. Popular with locals, walkers and other visitors to the area, this fine pub is a hub of village life. Built in the

1700s of local stone, it features some original elements - like the old wooden money drawer, the only till the pub has ever known. The open coal fire dates back to the 1800s. Prints and memorabilia of the days of the miners - old lamps, hel-

**The Kings Head, Coleford, nr Bath, Somerset BA3 5LU**
**Tel: 01373 812346**

mets and more - along with copper and brass pieces, china and porcelain adorn the walls. Antique chairs and oak tables add to the traditional atmosphere of the place - visitors will feel transported back to more gracious and friendly times. A home from home for one and all, the pub has a good range of real ales, spirits and soft drinks. All the food available is home-made, and includes pies, pasties, hearty sandwiches, rolls and more.

## SHEPTON MALLET

An important centre of communications since pre-Roman times, the old market town of Shepton Mallet lies on the River Sheppey, a little to the west of the **Fosse Way**, the old Roman route which at this point comprises a stretch of the modern A37. The settlement's Saxon name, which means simply "sheep town", reveals its main commercial activity during the pre-Norman and medieval periods, originally as a centre of wool production, and later as a weaving town. The industry reached its peak in the 15th century and it was then that Shepton Mallet's magnificent parish church was constructed. This striking building has one of the earliest Perpendicular towers in the county and a remarkable wagon roof with some 350 carved oak panels and around 300 bosses, each fashioned to a different design.

Perhaps Shepton Mallet's most characteristic structure, however, is its 50 foot **Market Cross**. Built around 1500 and restored in 1841, it has been the town's civic and commercial hub for almost 500 years. Indeed, a lively modern market continues to be held here every Friday. Several participants in the Duke of Monmouth's ill fated Pitchfork Rebellion were executed at the market cross in 1685 on the orders of the infamous Judge Jeffreys. The curious roofed structure standing nearby is a fixed market stall dating from the 15th century which is the only surviving remnant of Shepton's medieval butchers' market, or shambles. A lane running east off Town Street leads past the church to the old prison. Thought to be well away from the threat of enemy bombs, the Domesday Book was brought here for safe keeping during the Second World War.

On the edge of the town centre of Shepton Mallet, **Bowlish House** hotel and restaurant is the deserved recipient of numerous accolades from Egon Ronay and other professional organizations. This grand old house was built by a notable clothier of his day in the 1700s, and boasts a Palladian-style facade with six pairs of windows and central, pillared double door entrance up a short flight of steps. It served as a brewery for many years before again passing into private hands. In 1954 it began the latest phase of its history, as a distinguished hotel and restaurant. This listed Grade II building has an older wing, not visible from the front, which pre-dates the 1732 construction of the rest of this gracious house by some 50 years. Both the exterior and interior are in excellent condition, led by the concern of Stephen Clark (of Clarks shoes fame) who bought the property in 1964 and restored the buildings and grounds with great care and sensitivity. The lounge and separate bar are attractive and comfortable, just the places to enjoy a quiet drink, pre-dinner, after dinner or at any time. A small spring rises under the cellar, linking up with an underground stream which run under the old flagstones of the cellar floor. This helps to maintain the perfect temperature for the 200 bottles of wine kept here. Linen tablecloths and crystal glassware set the tone at this elegant establishment. The excellent menu includes an impressive range of culinary delights, such as, as an example fillet of beef with saffron glazed potatoes, filets of brill with lobster sauce served on a bed of taglioni, partridge breasts, and roasted Mediterranean vegetable gratin. The selections of desserts and fine English cheeses are also worth saving room for! There accommodation comprises three superior en suite bedrooms, notable for their stylish furnishings and fittings, and all supremely comfortable.

**Bowlish House and Restaurant, Wells Road, Shepton Mallet, Somerset BA4 5JD Tel/Fax: 01749 342022**

Present-day Shepton Mallet is a prosperous light industrial town which has a good selection of shopping and leisure facilities. One of its largest industrial employers is Showerings, the makers of Babycham. For those with an interest in the town's social and industrial past, it is well worth visiting the district museum at the top of the High Street. Each year, Shepton Mallet plays host to two well-established agricultural shows: the **Mid-Somerset Show**, which is held in the town on a Saturday in August, and the **Royal Bath and West Show**, which is held over four days at the end of May on a permanent site beside the A371, a couple of miles to the south of the town centre.

Tucked away at the western edge of Shepton Mallet, **The King William Inn** is an obvious favourite with locals and visitors alike. This attractive and welcoming inn dates back some 300 years and was created from three former stables, used when Shepton was home to the largest sheep market in England. Ancient timbers have been refurbished to make the long bar with the open plan interior, with comfortable settles, stools and sturdy tables. Prints, old photographs, copper plaques and cigarette cards adorn the walls, while the fire and other original features enhance the traditional and cosy ambience. A warm and friendly welcome awaits all guests. Roy and Melanie Farmer have been here since 1999; they bring enthusiasm and conscientiousness to the endeavour, and they and their staff make every

**The King William Inn, West Shepton, Shepton Mallet, Somerset BA4 5UG Tel: 01749 342102**

effort to ensure guests have a relaxing and pleasant time. Community spirit prevails here, evident in the informal atmosphere. Guests can join in on traditional games such as shove half-penny and others. Real ales are on tap, together with a wealth of other beverages including a good complement of wines and spirits, ciders and soft drinks. The delicious bar snacks and sandwiches make for a hearty repast. All in all this is an excellent place to stop for a break from touring the many sights and attractions of the area.

In 1995, Bronze Age homesteads and pottery were found during excavations near **Cannards Grave**, to the south of the town. **Maesbury Ring**, the Iron Age hillfort which crowns the northern horizon of the town, 950 feet up on the Mendips, is the earliest visible trace.

# AROUND SHEPTON MALLET

## LEIGH-UPON-MENDIP                                    MAP 2 REF H4
4 miles NE of Shepton Mallet off the A367

A lane to the south of Babington House leads to Leigh-upon-Mendip (pronounced lye), a sizable village whose church tower is modelled on its sister church at Mells. The interior, however, is less ornate, with a plain Norman font and simple pews.

The eastern terminus of the **East Somerset Railway** lies to the south of the A361 Frome to Shepton Mallet road, three miles to the southwest of Leigh-upon-Mendip in Cranmore. Originally a broad gauge line dating from the 1850s, the present steam railway was founded by the wildlife artist, David Shepherd, in 1975. Assisted by an enthusiastic team of volunteers, Shepherd has assembled an outstanding collection of steam locomotives, varying in size from the tiny *Lord Fisher* to the mighty *Black Prince*. The line runs for three miles to the terminus at Mendip Vale. An impressive replica Victorian engine shed and workshops have been built near Cranmore Station.

## DOULTING
MAP 2 REF H4

1 mile E of Shepton Mallet on the A361

Doulting is unusual in Somerset in that its church has a tall spire, rather than a tower. An imposing part 12th century building with a handsome exterior, it also has a splendid two storey porch which incorporates a curious carving of the green man into its vaulting; the church interior, however, is over-restored and disappointing. The village dates back to the 8th century when King Ine of Wessex gave the local estate to Glastonbury Abbey after his nephew, St Aldhelm, the Abbot of Malmesbury and first Bishop of Sherborne, died here in 709. The saint's body was carried back to Malmesbury along a circuitous route which was marked for posterity by a series of tall stone crosses. The church, a statue, and the spring in the former vicarage garden are all dedicated to St Aldhelm. The spring was later incorporated into a holy well which became a place of pilgrimage during the Middle Ages.

The 15th century **Tithe Barn** at the southern end of the village is a relic of Doulting's monastic past. This great building was constructed to store tithes, one tenth of the local tenant farmers' crops which they paid annually to their ecclesiastical landlords. Another important source of revenue came from the great quarry which lay to the north of the village. The fine cream-coloured stone from here was used in the construction of Wells Cathedral and for later additions to Glastonbury Abbey. The handsome terrace of estate-style cottages near the church is more recent, however, dating from the end of the Victorian era.

## STOKE ST MICHAEL
MAP 2 REF H4

2 miles NE of Shepton Mallet off the A367

**Stoke Bottom Farm** in Stoke St Michael is a working dairy farm set in 370 acres. Owner Christine Marks takes pride in providing guests of all nations (many return again and again) with superior bed and breakfast accommodation here in her lovely farmhouse home. There are two guest bedrooms (one twin, one double/family room), warm, comfortable and decorated and furnished to a high standard of quality. A welcoming family atmosphere pervades, making the ambience relaxing and informal. Typical Somerset hospitality is on hand, and the surrounding open countryside offers some superb walking.

Host to many visitors from diverse countries, touring Bath, Longleat, Wells and the many other sights and attractions of this part of Somerset and beyond, this distinctive place epitomizes the ideal rural retreat. Breakfasts are

**Stoke Bottom Farm, Stoke St Michael, nr Bath, Somerset BA3 5HW Tel: 01761 232273**

hearty and delicious, setting guests up for a day's walking or sightseeing.

## OAKHILL
Map 2 ref H4

2 miles N of Shepton Mallet on the A367

The old brewing village of Oakhill lies in the lanes to the north of this junction. Although the original brewery has long since disappeared, in recent years a new one has opened to provide the pubs and inns of the district with traditional ales. This is also the location of **Oakhill Manor**, a small country mansion set in an attractive 45 acre estate which has been developed as a popular visitor attraction. The car park is connected to the house by a scenic miniature railway which incorporates a scaled-down version of Cheddar Gorge, and the manor itself contains an extraordinary collection of models and pictures, mostly relating to historic forms of land, sea and air transport.

## STRATTON-ON-THE-FOSSE
Map 2 ref H4

5 miles N of Shepton Mallet on the A367

Three miles to the northeast of Oakhill, the A367 passes through Stratton-on-the-Fosse, a former coal-mining community which is also the home of the famous Roman Catholic boys' public school, **Downside Abbey**. The school occupies the site of a monastery which was founded in 1814 by a group of English Benedictines who had emigrated to France but were subsequently driven out by the French Revolution. The steady expansion of the school during the 20th century encouraged the monks to move to a new site on higher ground near the existing abbey church, an impressive building which took over 70 years to complete and numbered among its architects, Sir Giles Gilbert Scott.

Stratton-on-the Fosse also possesses a handsome parish church which stands on the opposite side of the A367. This striking part medieval building incorporates a number of 18th and 19th century features which were added at the time the local coal mining industry was at its peak. Hard to imagine today, Stratton is situated at the southern edge of the once prosperous, but now almost forgotten, Somerset coalfield. The last mine in the town was closed in 1968.

## CHEWTON MENDIP                                  Map 2 ref G3
5 miles NW of Shepton Mallet on the A39

One of the most celebrated cheese makers in the North Somerset can be found at Chewton Mendip, a village lying on the A39 Wells to Bath road, four miles to the west of Stratton-on-the-Fosse. **Chewton Cheese Dairy** at Priory Farm is one of the few remaining cheese-making dairies which still uses truly traditional methods. Here, the ancient art of preparing genuine Cheddar cheese can be observed at first hand.

## WEST HARPTREE                                   Map 2 ref G3
8 miles NW of Shepton Mallet off the A368/B3114

A mile from Chew Valley Lake, and handy for Bristol, Bath, Cheddar and other sights and attractions in the region, **The Crown Inn** is a distinguished 300-year-old coaching inn. This very attractive stonebuilt inn has a warm and relaxed atmosphere. The interior features a lounge and public bar, decorated and furnished in traditional style, with open fires in the bar. The walls are adorned with old photographs of local scenes, enhancing the cosy ambience.

To the rear there's an enclosed walled garden, complete with comfortable seating, barbecue and children's play area. Real ales, bottled and draught lagers, wines, spirits and

**The Crown Inn, High Street, West Harptree, Somerset BS40 6HA Tel: 01761 221432**

soft drinks are all on hand, and can be accompanied by a range of tasty bar snacks (available all day), freshly made sandwiches or ploughmans. Tenants Gerry and Melody Smart and their capable, helpful staff make every guest feel most welcome. Accommodation is available in one of two guest bedrooms (a double and a family room), each very comfortable and welcoming.

## CROSCOMBE                                              MAP 2 REF G4
2 miles W of Shepton Mallet on the A371

The former weaving village of Croscombe lies a couple of miles to the west of Shepton Mallet beside the A371 Wells road. Among the many fine stone buildings to be found here is the parish church, an imposing part 13th century building with a tall spire, a rarity in Somerset. The interior contains a magnificent collection of Jacobean dark oak fittings carved in a variety of heraldic and pastoral designs. The medieval manor house behind the church has recently been restored by the Landmark Trust.

## EVERCREECH                                             MAP 2 REF H4
3 miles SE of Shepton Mallet off the B3081

A church tower which is much more characteristic of the county can be found at Evercreech, an attractive village which lies on the B3081 Bruton road, a mile to the southeast of the Royal Bath and West showground. The impressive Perpendicular tower of **St Peter's**, with its multi-tiering, complex tracery and tall pinnacles, creates an impression of great height. Perhaps the most striking feature of the church interior is the ceiling of the nave, which is adorned with sixteen painted angels and a series of gilded roof bosses. The church overlooks a delightful square with a village cross which is surrounded by some lovely old stone cottages and almshouses.

## BATCOMBE                                               MAP 2 REF H4
4 miles SE of Shepton Mallet off the A32/A359

A lane to the east of Evercreech leads through the hamlet of Stony Stratton to Batcombe, a secluded community set within an Area of Outstanding Natural Beauty. The village, whose name means "Bata's valley" in Saxon, has one of the finest perpendicular Gothic church towers in Somerset. This was built in the 16th century when Batcombe was an important centre of the wool industry. Indeed, at that time the district's nine cloth mills were producing more woven material than those along the River Avon between Bath and Bristol.

Adjacent to the church of St Mary the Virgin in Batcombe, the distinguished **Three Horseshoes** public house and restaurant dates back to the 12th century, and is crafted from stone. Exposed beams and little alcoves heighten the old-world feel of this fine traditional pub. The open-plan bar area is warm and inviting, with a huge open log fire on colder days. The walls are adorned with

The Three Horseshoes, Batcombe,
nr Shepton Mallet, Somerset BA4 6HE
Tel: 01749 850359 Fax: 01749 850615
website: www.three-horseshoes.co.uk

an interesting collection of toby jugs and other mugs and tankards. A handsome stone archway marks the entrance to the separate "Coach House" restaurant, which boasts a high ceiling and is airy and spacious. Set at an angle to this main restaurant is a conservatory dining area as well. The comprehensive menu changes weekly, but guests are always sure to find an excellent range of expertly prepared and presented dishes such as breast of duck, steak and Guinness pie, guinea fowl, smoked salmon with pasta, and vegetarian choices. In addition there is a good variety of specials, and tempting desserts well worth leaving room for. The wine list is very good, and features a good many French, German, Chilean and Spanish vintages. This welcoming establishment is handy for Longleat, Bath, Wells, Glastonbury and many other of the region's attractions and sights. Open daily midday-3 and 6.30 to 11; open from 12 midday, Fridays and Saturdays.

EAST PENNARD                                     Map 2 ref G5
3 miles S of Shepton Mallet off the A37

A lane to the west of Evercreech leads across the A371 and A37 to the secluded village of East Pennard, the location of one of Britain's few organic wine producers. The **Avalon Vineyard** produces an attractive range of wines, ciders and mead, all from organically grown produce. The sheltered south-facing slopes of the southern Mendips have become popular with the new generation of English vine growers, most of which welcome visitors for tours and wine tastings.

PILTON                                           Map 2 ref G4
1 mile SW of Shepton Mallet off the A361

A fine example can be found at Pilton, a scattered village which lies just off the

A361 Shepton Mallet to Glastonbury road, two miles to the north of East Pennard. The extensive grounds of **Pilton Manor**, a former summer residence of the abbots of Glastonbury, have been planted with vines, mostly of the German Riesling variety, and visitors are invited to stroll around the estate and sample the end product. The present manor house is a curious combination of architectural styles: largely Georgian, its central Venetian-style window is surrounded by medieval-looking turrets, pinnacles and castellations.

Another legacy from the abbey is Pilton's great cruciform tithe barn which stands on a hill surrounded by beech and chestnut trees. Sadly, its magnificent arch-braced roof was destroyed when the building was struck by lightning in 1963. The roof of the parish church of St John has been more fortunate: considered a 15th century masterpiece, it has survived for over 500 years. This superb little building also has an impressive Norman south doorway with characteristic zigzag carving, some fine 15th century stained glass in the chancel, and a unique collection of early instruments which were used to provide the congregation with musical accompaniment prior to the arrival of the church organ.

WEST PENNARD                                             MAP 2 REF G4
4 miles SW of Shepton Mallet on the A361

Back on the main A361 Shepton Mallet to Glastonbury road, the village of West Pennard is the location of a small National Trust-owned property, the **West Pennard Court Barn**. This unusual five-bay barn dates from the 15th century and can be found in the lanes to the south of the village.

# 4 Central Somerset

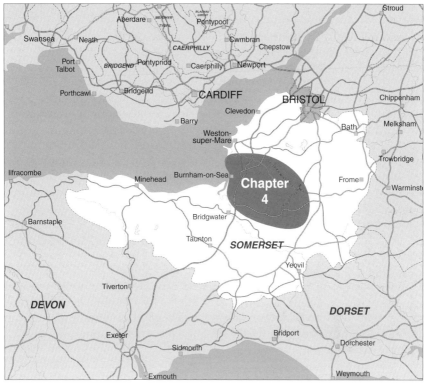

© MAPS IN MINUTES ™ (1998)

## GLASTONBURY

The ancient ecclesiastical centre of Glastonbury, a small town with an immense history, is a mecca for those encompassing such diverse beliefs as paganism, Christianity, Arthurian legend and the existence of UFOs. Before the surrounding Somerset Levels were drained in the 18th century, the dramatic form of **Glastonbury Tor** stood out above a great expanse of mist-covered marshland. Known throughout the region as the Isle of Avalon, one of the first outsiders to sail up the River Brue and land at this distinctive conical hill was the early Christian trader, Joseph of Arimathea, who arrived from the Holy Land around 60 AD. According to local legend, Joseph was walking one day on nearby Wearyall Hill when he plunged his staff into the ground. Miraculously, the stick took root and burst into leaf, and this he took as a sign he should found a church. A wattle and daub structure was duly erected at the spot which later became the site of the great **Glastonbury Abbey**.

Joseph's staff is reputed to have grown into the celebrated Christmas-flowering Glastonbury hawthorn, and although the original is believed to have been felled during Cromwellian times by an overzealous Puritan (he was blinded by a flying shard of wood in the process, no doubt as a gesture of retribution), one of its windswept descendants can still be seen on the crest of Wearyall Hill. In an extended version of the legend, Joseph was accompanied on one of his visits to Glastonbury by his nephew, the young Jesus Christ, an occurrence which is reputed to have provided William Blake with the inspiration for his hymn, Jerusalem.

Glastonbury Tor remains a landmark which can be seen from miles around, although curiously, it is often less conspicuous when viewed from close by. The 520 foot hill has been inhabited since prehistoric times, and excavations on the site have uncovered evidence of Celtic, Roman and pre-Saxon occupation. Because of its unusually regular shape, it has long been associated with myth and legend. For example, in its time it has been identified as the Land of the Dead, the Celtic Otherworld, a Druid's temple, magic mountain, Arthurian hillfort, ley line intersection, and rendezvous point for passing UFOs.

Along with mystical energy, the tor offers a magnificent panorama across Somerset to Wells, the Mendips, the Quantocks and the Bristol Channel. The view from the top is most breathtaking on a misty day when the Tor is surrounded by a sea of silver cloud. The striking tower at the summit is all that remains of the 15th century **Church of St Michael**, an offshoot of Glastonbury Abbey which fell into disrepair following the Dissolution of the Monasteries in 1539. In that turbulent year, the tor became a place of execution when the last abbot of Glastonbury, Richard Whiting, and two of his monks were hanged near the summit for opposing the will of Henry VIII.

**Glastonbury Tor**

The wooded rise standing between Glastonbury Tor and the town centre is known as **Chalice Hill**. During one of his visits in the 1st century AD, Joseph of Arimathea is supposed to have buried the Holy Grail (the cup used by Christ at the Last Supper) beneath a spring which emerges from the foot of the hill's southern slope. The spring forms a natural well which was partially enclosed within a masonry structure during medieval times. This is now situated in an attractive garden maintained by the **Chalice Well Trust**. The spring water has a high iron content which leaves a curious rust-coloured (some say blood-coloured) residue in its wake. It is also reputed to have curative powers and flows at a constant rate of 25,000 gallons per day into a pool known as the Pilgrim's Bath.

The dramatic remains of **Glastonbury Abbey** can be found to the northwest of Chalice Hill in the heart of old Glastonbury. If the legend of Joseph of Arimathea is to be believed, this is the site of the earliest Christian foundation in the British Isles. The abbey is thought to have been founded by King Ine around 700 AD, and under St Dunstan, the 10th century abbot who went on to become the Archbishop of Canterbury, it grew in influence so that by the time of the Norman invasion, it owned estates covering an eighth of the county of Somerset. The abbey continued to grow under the guidance of the Benedictines until a disastrous fire destroyed most of the abbey buildings in 1184.

**Glastonbury Abbey**

When the foundations of the replacement great church were being excavated seven years later, a wooden sarcophagus was discovered 16 feet down between the shafts of two ancient crosses. Inside were found the bones of a large man and a slender woman, and one story tells of how the woman's long golden hair seemed in a perfect state of preservation until a monk touched it, transforming it to dust. A lead cross found nearby convinced the abbot that he had discovered the remains of King Arthur and Queen Guinevere, although it was known at the time that this was the burial place of at least three kings from the later, Saxon period.

The abbot's discovery could well be described as timely, given his pressing need for funds to pay for the abbey's reconstruction. Notwithstanding, Glastonbury soon became an important place of pilgrimage, and when the main part of the abbey had been completed in 1278, King Edward himself arrived to witness the final re-interring of Arthur's bones in a magnificent new tomb in the choir. The regenerated great church was a massive 560 feet in length, with a splendid central bell-tower, twin west towers, a unique clock, and a series of shrines to the great and the good.

The abbey continued to wield considerable power until Henry VIII's Dissolution of the Monasteries of 1539 forced it to close. The building was abandoned and soon fell into disrepair: its walls were plundered for building stone and Arthur's tomb was destroyed. A number of impressive remains have nevertheless survived, the best-preserved being **St Mary's Chapel**, the shell of the great church, and the 14th century **Abbot's Kitchen**. The last named is a charming structure with a vaulted roof and a fireplace in each corner which has survived almost intact. The new visitors centre houses an excellent museum whose exhibits include a selection of historic artefacts from the site and a model of the abbey as it was at the time of the Dissolution.

**Abbey Tea Rooms and Licensed Restaurant** is a charming and welcoming establishment set in the heart of Glastonbury, adjacent to the Abbey and close to other Tor attractions. This handsome and comfortable restaurant was originally built in the 13th century of traditional materials. It presents a welcoming exterior to the world, with tall casement windows and pristine white paintwork over the stone facade. The interior features a welcoming open fire at one end which separates the kitchens from the rest of the room. The lighting is subdued and the decor is tasteful, adding to the cosy ambience. Porcelain and china ornaments adorn the three main walls, the lower part of which are fashioned of exposed stone while the upper part is decorated with charming flowered wallpaper. The Tudor-style wall plate timber beams are adorned with prints and photographs of local scenes. The restaurant is open daily for morning coffees, lunchtime meals and traditional Somerset cream teas. The extensive menu offers a range of delicious home-cooked and

Abbey Tea Rooms & Licensed Restaurant,
16 Magdalene Street, Glastonbury,
Somerset BA6 9EH Tel: 01458 832852

home-prepared dishes; there are also daily specials. A sample from the menu includes tempting sandwiches, hearty salads and home-made soup of the day, together, of course, with a superb range of mouth-watering cakes, scones, crumpets and teacakes. Meals can be complemented with hot or cold drinks, including specialist coffees, a variety of teas, mineral water, soft drinks, lager, cider, sherry or wine. There is also a children's menu. The staff are attentive and friendly, helping to make this restaurant the ideal place to stop for a relaxing and delicious break while sightseeing in Glastonbury and the surrounding area.

The abbey's principal **Tithe Barn** stands on its own to the southeast of the main monastic buildings. Although it is relatively small for such a great estate, it incorporates some fine sculptured detail, notably the carved heads on the corner buttresses and emblems of the four Evangelists on the gables.

The fine **Somerset Rural Life Museum** in Glastonbury is housed in a Victorian farmhouse and associated farm buildings, including the impressive 14th-century barn of Glastonbury Abbey. Exploring rural life in the country during the 19th and early 20th century, it offers a wealth of displays illustrating traditional farming practices and local industries such as peat-cutting, cheese- and cider-making, and withy-growing. In the cider apple orchard, visitors can see the museum's apiary and rare breeds of farm animals. A glimpse into the past is on show in the original Victorian farmhouse kitchen, fully equipped with all the wares, crockery, cutlery and furnishings of the time. The story of 19th-century farm labourer John Hodges

Somerset Rural Life Museum, Abbey Farm,
Chilkwell Street, Glastonbury  BA6 8DB
Tel: 01458 831197  Fax: 01458 834684
e-mail: county-museums@somerset.gov.uk
website: www.somerset.gov.uk/museums

and his family is vividly retold. There's a changing programme of fascinating events and demonstrations throughout the year, such as displays of traditional farming methods and crafts. Events past and present for children and adults have included demonstrations by the West Country Potters Association, an exhibition of sculptures by local artists, pottery and farmhouse cookery workshops, plant sales, Easter egg hunts, cider-making weekends, West Country craft fairs, and Living History Weekends where historical groups such as The 1685 Society re-enact great moments in Somerset history. The museum shop stocks a good range of crafts, books and memorabilia, while the attractive tea room (open late March to the end of September and during the October half-term holidays) serves delicious refreshments. For a truly interesting and stimulating experience, and a chance to learn in a fun and relaxed atmosphere, this excellent museum is well worth a visit. Open: 1st April to 31st October, Tuesday - Friday and Bank Holiday Mondays 10-5, Saturday and Sunday 2-6; November to end March Tuesday to Saturday 10-3. Admission to the museum also allows the visitor entrance to the Somerset County Museum in Taunton.

**Norwood Park Farm** is within a short distance of Glastonbury Tor, with the Rural Life Museum nearby and within easy reach of Wells, Glastonbury and other intriguing and lovely sights of the surrounding area. Set within 260 acres, the main farmhouse is distinctive and impressive, a traditional stonebuilt structure created by Abbot John De Selwode as a Retreat House for the Abbots of Glastonbury in the 15th century. There are two comfortable, spacious and welcoming guest bedrooms. One room boasts a lovely four-poster bed. Original features such as timber-planked doors, stone mullion windows and open fireplaces are combined with modern amenities to offer guests a high standard of comfort and quality. The guests' lounge is particularly welcoming and comfortable. Interesting architectural features include the coat of arms carved in the stone on the outside wall. Period furniture enhances the homely, traditional ambience. Owners Anne and Philip Saunders are relaxed and informal hosts, who enjoy making guests feel very welcome. The country farmhouse breakfast is delicious and plentiful.

**Norwood Park Farm, Wick, Glastonbury, Somerset BA6 8JS Tel/Fax: 01458 831979 e-mail: norwoodpk@hotmail.com**

During the Middle Ages, Glastonbury Abbey was an internationally renowned centre of learning which attracted scholars and pilgrims from all over Christendom. Such were the eventual numbers that a guesthouse had to be built outside the abbey walls. Originally constructed around 1475, the much ornamented **George and Pilgrims Hotel** can still be seen in the High Street near the Market Cross. The old timber beams of this striking building are adorned with carved angels and the fireplace in the bar is surrounded by Delft tiles which are over two centuries old. The interior is guarded by a series of curious monks' death masks, and at one time, the building was even rumoured to have a subterranean passage leading from the cellar into the abbey grounds. A couple of doors away, **The Tribunal**, a handsome early 15th-century building, now houses the tourist information office. The two square panels above the doorway each contain the royal emblem of the Tudors. Among the many fine churches to be found in Glastonbury are **St John's Baptist church** in the High Street, which has an imposing 134ft tower, and St Mary's Roman Catholic church in Magdalene Street, which dates from the outbreak of the Second World War.

**The Lightship and Christmas Cottage, 82 Bovetown, Glastonbury, Somerset BA6 8JG Tel: 01458 833698**

Anyone seeking peace, tranquillity and a relaxed and informal atmosphere should look no further than **The Lightship and Christmas Cottage** in Glastonbury. Tucked away in "above town", Glastonbury, within a mile of the Tor, it is within easy reach of Wells, Bath and Somerton. Visitors to the Tor and its associated places of pilgrimage are made most welcome here. Owner Rose Sananda is a writer, healer and folk musician. She has lived here since 1988 and organises her life around her writing and her guests. There are two cosy and charming rooms available, as well as self-catering accommodation in the adjoining Christmas Cottage. Dating back to the 1400s, The Lightship house and Christmas Cottage offer a wealth of beautiful original features combined with modern amenities. Aromatherapy, massage, spiritual healing and other holistic treatments are available to all guests. The warmth and welcoming ambience of this unique establishment are well worth seeking out.

A National Trust footpath to the east of Glastonbury leads to **Gog and Magog**, the ancient oaks of Avalon. This famous pair of living antiquities are all that remain of an avenue of oaks which, sadly, was cut down in the 1900s to make way for a farm. One of the felled trees was eleven feet in diameter and was recorded as having over 2000 season rings.

Another historic place of interest can be found to the northwest of Glastonbury town centre in a field beside the road to Godney. This was the site of a prehistoric **Lake Village** which was discovered in 1892 when it was noticed that a section of an otherwise level site was studded with irregular mounds. Thought to date from around 150 BC, the dwellings were built on a series of tall platforms which raised them above the surrounding marshland. An interesting collection of artefacts recovered from the site can be seen in the town museum.

In its time, Glastonbury has been called the Ancient Avalon, the New Jerusalem, and the "Holyest Erthe" in England. It is a place of natural enchantment which attracts an ever-growing number of pilgrims of the new age who are drawn by its unique landscape, atmosphere and quality of light.

One of the greatest mysteries of the locality, indeed one which may possess something of a credibility gap, is difficult to observe except from the air. Much loved and eagerly propounded by those with an interest in astrology, the **Glastonbury Zodiac** was brought to light in 1935 by Katherine Maltwood when she was researching a book on the Holy Grail. According to Maltwood, the 12 signs of the zodiac appear in their correct order as recognisable features of the landscape, their outlines being delineated by streams, tracks, ridges and ancient boundaries. The entire formation lies within a circle with a seven mile radius whose centre lies three miles to the south of Glastonbury near the village of Butleigh. Its origins remain a subject of speculation.

# AROUND GLASTONBURY

MEARE                                                              Map 2 ref F4
3 miles NW of Glastonbury on the B3151

The attractive village of Meare lies three miles along the B3151 Wedmore road to the northwest of Glastonbury. When approaching the village from the east, an unusual medieval building known as the **Abbot's Fish House** can be seen on the northern side of the main road. Prior to about 1700, this isolated structure stood on the edge of **Meare Pool**, a substantial lake over a mile and a half in diameter which provided Glastonbury abbey with a regular supply of freshwater fish. Before the lake was drained, this plain, early 14th-century building was used for storing fishing equipment and salting fish. It has three ground-floor and two first-floor rooms, the upper level being reached by way of an external staircase.

Rising to only 30 feet above sea level, the surrounding **Somerset Levels** cover an extensive area bordered by the Mendips to the northeast, the Quantocks to the west, and Ham-stone country to the south. For thousands of years, this low-lying stretch of countryside spent much of the year submerged under a layer of standing water, conditions ideal for the formation of peat, which is created when a lack of oxygen prevents the normal decomposition of vegetation. Piecemeal channels had been dug for centuries, but it was only in the last quarter of the 18th century that a coordinated drainage system was proposed which included the construction of the great **King's Sedgemoor Drain** of 1794. As a result, the Levels are now crisscrossed by a complex system of artificial waterways which, in ascending order of size, are known as ditches, rhines (pronounced reens) and drains. This fascinating area contains a rich diversity of wildlife and has much to offer the walker, bird-watcher, rural historian and casual visitor.

## WESTHAY                                                        Map 2 ref F4
4 miles NW of Glastonbury on the B3151

At Westhay, a mile and a half to the west of Meare, the **Peat Moor Visitor Centre** offers a fascinating insight into the history and ecology of the Somerset Levels. A series of imaginatively presented displays describe the development of commercial peat digging through the ages, the special trades which have grown up in this unique environment, and the measures which have been taken to conserve the area's flora and fauna. There is also a reconstruction of a section of the oldest manmade walkway in the world, the "Sweet Track." Thought to date from around 4000 BC, the original was constructed of hewn timbers and ran across the Levels from the Polden ridge to the Isle of Westhay.

## STREET                                                         Map 2 ref G5
1 mile SW of Glastonbury on the A39

Historic Glastonbury has long been a conservation area whose growth has been severely restricted. No such restrictions, however, have applied to Street, a sprawling town lying a couple of miles to the southwest of Glastonbury whose population now approaches 10,000. A surprisingly old settlement which takes its name from the rebuilding of the causeway between Street and Glastonbury in the late 12th century. The oldest part is centred around the part 14th century parish **Church of the Holy Trinity**. Most of the town, however, dates from the 19th century when it began to grow from a small rural village to the modern light industrial centre which can be seen today. The dramatic expansion was largely due to one entrepreneurial Quaker family, the Clarks. In the 1820s, Cyrus and James Clark began producing sheepskin slippers from the hides of local animals, and over the following century-and-a-half, their firm grew into one the largest manufacturers of quality shoes in Europe.

Many of the older buildings in Street owe their existence to the family, including the **Friends' Meeting House** of 1850, the clock tower, and the building which housed the original Millfield School. (The main part of the school has been relocated to the outskirts of the town.) The oldest part of the Clark's factory has now been converted into a fascinating footwear museum containing displays of historic shoes, shoe-making machinery, fashion photographs and exhibits chronicling the history of shoe design from Roman times to the present day. The company's headquarters are still located in Street, along with one of the first purpose-built factory shopping centres in Britain, the Clark's Village.

## BUTLEIGH WOOTTON                                       MAP 2 REF G5
3 miles SE of Glastonbury off the B3151

The conspicuous columnar monument which can be seen on the ridge above Butleigh Wootton, a couple of miles to the southeast of Street, is dedicated to Vice Admiral Sir Samuel Hood, a member of the celebrated family of naval officers who won a string of important maritime victories during the second half of the 18th century. **Butleigh Court** in Butleigh is an impressive Victorian pile built in 1845 which was damaged by fire and later divided into separate residential units.

## COMPTON DUNDON                                         MAP 2 REF G5
4 miles S of Glastonbury off the A361/B3151

Located opposite the beautiful local church of St Andrew, **Church Farm Guest House** is a thatched period cottage, which has been renovated and refurbished **to** provide every modern amenity while retaining its traditional appeal. There are five superior en suite guest bedrooms, all furnished and decorated to a high standard of comfort and quality. Set amid mature gardens of lawns, shrubs, roses and borders, including an area set aside as a tea garden, parts of this distinctive farmhouse are 400 years old. The low beamed ceilings, natural stone walls,

**Church Farm Guest House, Compton Dundon, nr Somerton, Somerset TA11 6PE  Tel: 01458 272927**

open fireplaces and numerous nooks and crannies speak of a bygone age; all the furnishings are in period style, and the walls are adorned with fascinating prints and local photographs. The rooms are spacious and very confortable, commanding superb views in all directions. This quintessentially English country home is the ideal place to relax and unwind. The breakfasts offer a wealth of delicious options, including home-baked breads and jams. Evening meals are available at this fully licensed establishment.

Set amid extensive enclosed gardens, **Castlebrook Holiday Cottages** are two fully equipped holiday homes located in the heart of the Polden Hills. Recently fully refurbished, each of the two cottages was named centuries ago after local fields. The first, Pool Hay, sleeps five, with a double, single and twin bedroom, comfortable sitting/dining room and well-appointed kitchen and shower room/WC. The upstairs rooms of this charming cottage overlook the orchard. The second cottage is called Press Bars. This sleeps three, in one double and one

**Castlebrook Holiday Cottages, Compton Dundon, Somerton, Somerset TA11 6PR Tel: 01458 841680**

single bedroom. Downstairs in this cosy cottage there's a lovely sitting/dining room with feature fireplace, kitchenette and shower room/WC. Both cottages have wooden stairs made from timber reclaimed from Taunton County Cricket Ground and Weston-super-Mare pier. National Trust properties and places to visit nearby include Dundon Beacon (an Iron Age fort), Gilling Down, Ivythorne Hill, Hood Monument and much more besides. The cottages are also within easy reach of Cheddar, Wells, Glastonbury and Bath. All in all, they make the perfect relaxing retreat while remaining accessible to local sights and attractions of interest.

## BALTONSBOROUGH
3 miles SE of Glastonbury off the A361

MAP 2 REF G5

Baltonsborough was the birthplace of St Dunstan, one of the greatest figures in the Anglo-Saxon church who rose to become abbot of Glastonbury Abbey and then Archbishop of Canterbury.  A fine example of a medieval church house adjoins the parish churchyard; a rarity in Somerset, it once served the community as a brewery and village hall.

## SHAPWICK
Map 2 ref F5

4 miles W of Glastonbury off the A39

The A39 to the west of Street runs along the crest of the Polden Hills, a long low ridge which, despite rising to less than 300 feet, seems to dominate the surrounding countryside. Like everything else in this strange heathland landscape, the roads here are built on peat, giving them a curious spongy feel. The terrain around the village of Shapwick is scarred by an extensive peat-digging operation which over the years has extracted great quantities of this natural soil conditioner for use in suburban gardens. Nearby **Shapwick Heath Nature Reserve** provides a safe haven for rare plants and wildlife, although to enter, it is necessary to obtain a permit from the Nature Conservancy Council in Taunton. No such restrictions apply to the public footpath which sets out across undamaged moor to the northwest of the village.

## MOORLINCH
Map 2 ref F5

5 miles SW of Glastonbury off the A39

The remote community of Moorlinch lies on the southern side of the A39, two miles to the southwest of Shapwick. This is the location of the **Moorlynch Vineyard**, an attractively situated 16 acre vineyard which offers wine tastings and tours of the winery.

## WESTONZOYLAND
Map 2 ref F5

7 miles SW of Glastonbury on the A372

The site of the last battle to be fought on English soil lies on the southern bank of what is now the **King's Sedgemoor Drain**, three miles to the southeast of Bawdrip, between Glastonbury and Bridgwater. In July 1685, a field to the north of the village of Westonzoyland was the location of the Battle of Sedgemoor, a bloody encounter in which the well-equipped forces of King James II defeated the followers of the Duke of Monmouth to bring to an end the ill-fated "Pitchfork Rebellion". Around 700 of Monmouth's followers were slaughtered on the battlefield, and several hundred more were rounded up and taken to the churchyard at Westonzoyland where many were hanged. The Duke himself was taken to London where, ten days after the battle, he was executed on Tower Hill. However, it was during the infamous Judge Jeffreys' "Bloody Assizes" that the greatest terror was inflicted: well over 300 men were condemned to death and summarily executed, and another 600 transported to the colonies. Today, the lonely battlefield is marked by a stark memorial.

Westonzoyland is also the site of an interesting steam-powered **Pumping Station** which was built in Victorian times to pump water into the River Parrett.

The oldest of its kind in the Somerset Levels, the current engine, which replaced an earlier version dating from the 1830s, was in operation from 1861 to 1952. It has now been fully restored, entirely by volunteer labour, and is now Grade II star listed. The main engine can be seen in steam at various times throughout the year (the Tourist Information Centre in Glastonbury will have the details). The site incorporates a small forge, a tramway and a number of exhibits from the age of steam.

## BURROW BRIDGE
MAP 2 REF F5
8 miles SW of Glastonbury off the A361

Another interesting pumping station can be seen beside the River Parrett at Burrow Bridge, three miles to the south of Westonzoyland. It also contains a fine collection of Victorian pump engines and is open to the public on certain days each year. Burrow Bridge is also the location of the **Somerset Levels Basket and Craft Centre**, a workshop and showroom stocked with handmade basketware.

The conspicuous conical hill which can be seen nearby is known as **Burrow Mump**. This isolated knoll is reputed to be the site of an ancient fort belonging to King Alfred, the 9th century King of Wessex, who is thought to have re-

**Burrow Mump Fort**

treated to this lonely spot to escape a Viking incursion. It was during his time here that he is rumoured to have sought shelter in a hut in the nearby village of Athelney and was scolded by the family for burning their cakes. In many ways reminiscent of Glastonbury Tor, Burrow Mump is crowned by the picturesque remains of an unfinished attempt to rebuild the chapel which began in 1793 but for which the funds ran out before its completion. These can be seen from miles around. Burrow Mump is situated in the heart of the low-lying area known as the **King's Sedge Moor**, an attractive part of the Somerset Levels which is drained by the rivers Cary (here renamed the King's Sedgemoor Drain) and Parrett. This rich area of wetland is known for its characteristic pollarded willows whose straight shoots, or withies, have been cultivated on a substantial scale ever since the taste for wicker developed during the Victorian era. The traditional craft of basket-making, one of Somerset's oldest commercial activities, once employed thousands of people. Though now very much scaled down, the industry is still alive and well and is even enjoying something of a revival.

## STOKE ST GREGORY                              Map 2 ref F5
### 10 miles SW of Glastonbury off the A361

Situated two and a half miles to the southwest of Burrow Mump, the village of Stoke St Gregory is the centre of Somerset's present-day wicker industry. Visitors to the **Willows and Wetlands Centre** can view the process of changing willow into finished baskets and wicker furniture. After the withies are cut, cleaned and boiled, they are woven into a wide variety of items using traditional methods which have been handed down for generations. Withies also provide the raw material for artist's charcoal. The centre contains a number of displays showing how the present Sedgemoor landscape has been created from marsh and swamp. It also has information on the many wild flowers, insects and birds which inhabit this unique wetland habitat.

# WELLS

The ancient ecclesiastical centre of Wells lies five miles along the A39 to the northeast of Glastonbury. With a population of under 10,000, this is the smallest city in England, and were it not for its cathedral and neighbouring bishop's palace, it would be unlikely to be more than an attractive small market town. However, the magnificent **Cathedral of St Andrew**, the first entirely Gothic structure of its kind in Britain, and its adjacent cathedral close, undoubtedly make this one of the gems of north Somerset.

Deriving its name from a line of springs which rise from the base of the Mendips, King Ine of the West Saxons is believed to have founded the first church at Wells around 700 AD. After a diocesan tussle with Bath, the present cathedral was begun in the 12th century and took over three

**Wells Cathedral**

centuries to complete. As a consequence, it demonstrates the three main styles of Gothic architecture - Early English, Decorated and Perpendicular. Its 13th century west front is generally considered to be its crowning glory: although defaced during the English Civil War, it incorporates over 100 larger-than-life-size statues of saints, angels and prophets who gaze down silently onto the cathedral lawn. The building's twin west towers were added a couple of centuries later; curious squat structures, they look as if they would benefit from the addition of spires.

The cathedral's many superb internal features include the beautiful and ingenious scissor arches which support the central tower, the great 14th century stained glass window over the high altar, the sweeping chapter house staircase with its elegant branching steps, and the great 14th century **Astronomical Clock**, one of the oldest working timepieces in the world. This shows the minutes, hours and phases of the moon on separate inner and outer dials, and marks the quarter hours with a lively mechanised knights' tournament.

The Cloister Restaurant,
Wells Cathedral, Wells, Somerset
BA5 2PA  Tel/Fax: 01749 676543

As its name tells us, **The Cloister Restaurant** in Wells is set in the original stone cloister of the splendid Cathedral. The inviting aroma of home-cooked foods greets visitors as they step into the light and airy quartile of the cloister. Here in these awe-inspiring surroundings, this counter service restaurant serves morning coffee, lunch and afternoon teas, including tempting sandwiches, delicious homemade cakes and superb main courses. Food is freshly prepared on the premises. The selection of main courses includes Somerset pork and apple casserole, cauliflower and Stilton flan, seasonal salads and hearty soups. The restaurant overlooks the Palm Churchyard and offers uninterrupted views of the full Cloister range and the south side of the Cathedral. Open: Monday - Saturday 10-5; Sunday 12.30-5. Winter closing: 4.30. Closed Good Friday, Christmas Day and Boxing Day. Catering for parties and functions can be arranged, to be held either here in the restaurant (for up to 84 guests) or in the 14th-century Vicars' Hall (up to 72 diners or 100 for a buffet).

The 52-acre cathedral close is a tranquil city within a city. Indeed for many centuries, Wells functioned as two distinct entities: the ecclesiastical city and civic city. The west front of the Cathedral is provided with an internal passage with pierced apertures and there is a theory that choirboys might have sung through these to give the illusion to those gathered on the Cathedral Green that the then lifelike painted statues were themselves singing. The green itself is surrounded by a high wall which is breached at only three castellated entrance points. One of these sturdy gateways stands in the corner of the Market Place; known as **Penniless Porch**, it is where the bishop allowed the poor of the city to beg for alms from visitors entering the cathedral, a custom which appears to be back in fashion today.

The **Vicars' Close**, one of the oldest planned streets in Europe, lies on the northern side of the cathedral green. This remarkable cobbled thoroughfare was built in the mid 14th century, although the ornate chimneys were added a century later. Originally intended for the adult

**Vicars' Close, Wells**

choristers called the Vicars Choral, it is still occupied by officers of the cathedral. The close is connected to the cathedral by a bridge which leads directly from the Vicars' Hall to the chapter house stairs. Known as the **Chain Gate**, it was built so that the innocent cathedral clergymen could avoid having to run the gauntlet of temptation by having to cross one of the town streets. (In a similar vein, the name of a thoroughfare in the town's former red light district was changed by the easily-affronted Victorians from Grope Lane to Union Street.)

The fortified **Bishop's Palace** is situated in an adjoining site to the south of the cathedral cloisters. This remarkable medieval building is surrounded by a moat which is fed by the springs which give the city its name. The palace is enclosed within a high stone wall, and in order to gain access from the Market Place, it is necessary to pass under a 13th century arch known as the **Bishop's Eye** and then cross a drawbridge which was last raised for defensive purposes in 1831. Although still the official residence of the Bishop of Bath and Wells, several parts are open to visitors, including the bishop's chapel and Jocelin's hall. The wide palace moat is home to a family of swans which are renowned for their ability to ask for food by ringing a bell on the wall below the gatehouse window. The impressive **Bishop's Tithe Barn** is situated to the south of the Bishop's Palace; in its day, it has served as a billet for royalist soldiers during the Bloody Assizes in 1685 and is now used for private functions.

Other noteworthy buildings in Wells include the part 15th century parish **Church of St Cuthbert**, which has such a lofty tower it is sometimes mistaken for the cathedral, and **Llewellyn's Almshouses** in Priest's Row. Founded 1614 and rebuilt between 1887 and 1901, these were originally constructed at the bequest of Henry Llewellyn who left £1600 to house "ten elderly women".

For those keen to find out more about the history of the locality, **Wells Museum**, near the west front of the cathedral, contains an interesting collection of locally-found artefacts. The splendid Cathedral Library possesses a number of rare books and manuscripts, a selection of which are on open display. The Market Place still hosts a lively street market on Wednesdays and Saturdays, or for those wanting a view of the city from a distance, an attractive footpath starts from Moat Walk and leads up onto the summit of Tor Hill.

**The Crown at Wells** is a 15th-century hotel and restaurant overlooking the medieval Market Place. The hotel is a Grade II listed building, with many traditional features. A range of comfortable accommodation is available, including

family rooms and rooms with four-poster beds. All 15 en suite bedrooms are attractively furnished in keeping with the hotel's 15th-century character. The hotel's popular restaurant is called Anton's Bistrot, named after a local well-known cartoonist whose work featured regularly in *Punch* magazine. Some of his original drawings adorn the walls of this stylish restaurant. The menu

**The Crown at Wells, Market Place, Wells, Somerset BA5 2RP Tel: 01749 673457  Fax: 01749 679792 e-mail: reception@crownwells.demon.co.uk**

offers a tempting variety of dishes. The delicious desserts are well worth saving room for. All meals can be accompanied by a selection from the superb wine list. The hotel's comfortable Penn Bar is the place to enjoy a relaxing drink, light meal or snack. The bar takes its name from William Penn, renowned Quaker and founder of Pennsylvania, who in 1685 once preached to the crowded market place from an upper window of the hotel. The Grape & Bean is an espresso and wine bar adjoining the Penn, offering a selection of pastries, Continental breakfasts and more available throughout the day. At weekend evenings a range of cocktails is served. The Outdoor Café is open on fine days for a variety of mouth-watering al fresco appetisers, accompanied by live music in the Market Place every Friday evening in July and August.

# SOUTH OF WELLS

## DINDER

MAP 2 REF G4

1 mile SE of Wells off the A371

Over 600 feet above sea level on the edge of Wells and Shepton Mallet, **Crapnell Farm** is a traditional 16th-century Grade II listed farmhouse offering bed and breakfast accommodation. Set in 240 acres of a working beef/arable farm, there are stunning views over the surrounding fields and pastures. There are many lovely original features which add to the old world feel of the place, such as the planked doors, gently sloping floors and intimate nooks and crannies. The original dumb waiter is also still intact, once used to transport cheeses up to the loft for curing.

**Crapnell Farm, Dinder, nr Wells, Somerset BA5 3HG
Tel: 01749 342683**

There are three charming and comfortable guest bedrooms, which capture the atmosphere of a traditional country home. The attractive guests' lounge and dining room are furnished in period style. The hearty breakfast will tempt every guest. Sandy and Pam Keen are friendly and welcoming hosts. This wonderful B&B makes an excellent base from which to explore this part of Somerset, and is in itself a peaceful and relaxing home from home.

## GODNEY                                                          Map 2 ref G4
### 6 miles SW of Wells off the A39/B3161

Just three miles north of Glastonbury, and six miles to the southwest of Wells, Godney is a small village with a great deal to offer. The River Sheppey and a plethora of natural and man-made beauties in the region makes this a perfect place to stop en route or to use as a base from which to explore the area.

Self-catering accommodation of a very comfortable standard is available at **Manor Farm** in Godney, in the heart of the Somerset Levels. A working dairy farm, it is family run and supports a herd of 80 dairy cows. Donkeys, goats, pigmy goats, wildfowl and other small farm animals wander the farm, and there is also a lovely and extensive garden. Visitors are welcome to explore the farm and observe the milking and other farm chores as they happen. The accommodation, in

**Manor Farm, Godney, nr Wells, Somerset  BA5 1RZ
Tel: 01458 834060**

a lovely cottage that is part of the main house, comprises two bedrooms (one double, one twin), bathroom with shower, a fully equipped kitchen (including washing machine) and modern, well-furnished lounge. An extra single bed can be provided upon request, as well as a cot or high chair. This ETM-commended accommodation is run by Cheiron and Martin Heal, who are friendly and helpful hosts. It makes an excellent base from which to explore Wells, Glastonbury, Cheddar and all the other sights and attractions within easy reach of this part of Somerset.

**Avalon Barn** in the small village of Godney is a charming and very comfortable home offering bed and breakfast accommodation. Of modern construction in traditional style, the handsome exterior is part-brick, part-stonebuilt; the interior is furnished in country cottage style. This welcoming establishment has an attractive guests' lounge. The three lovely and spacious guest bedrooms command superb views over the Somerset levels to the Mendips. Each room is individually furnished and decorated to a high standard of comfort and style. The

**Avalon Barn, Godney, Wells, Somerset BA5 1RZ**
**Tel/Fax: 01458 835005/835636**

breakfasts are hearty and varied - just the thing to set guests up for a day's sightseeing, or taking part in birdwatching (at nearby Westhay Bird Reserve), coarse fishing (in local rivers and ponds, practically from the front door), walking or cycling available in the area. There are several good local inns for evening meals. Owners Elaine and Gary Nicholls are welcoming, friendly and helpful hosts.

## NORTH AND WEST OF WELLS

### WEST HORRINGTON
3 miles NE of Wells off the A39/B3139

MAP 2 REF G4

The **Slab House Inn** in West Horrington was given its unusual name during the time of the Black Death, when a three-mile quarantine limit was imposed around Wells. Cautious farmers and traders would leave food, drink and other produce on a large slab outside the inn, to be collected by the people of Wells. All these centuries later, the inn is renowned for its excellent menu. A full a la carte menu is available at lunchtime and evening seven days a week, and features such delights as steaks, pork tenderloin, breaded scampi, rack of lamb, fillet of salmon, roast duck, fillet of beef and a good range of vegetarian dishes including mush-

**The Slab House Inn, Wells to Emborough Road, West Horrington, nr Wells, Somerset BA5 3EQ Tel: 01749 840310 Fax: 01749 840358**

room stroganoff and spinach and goat's cheese pancake. Bar snacks are also on offer lunch and evenings Monday to Thursday, at lunch only Fridays and Saturdays and evenings only on Sunday. Popular with locals and visitors alike, including those enjoying the excellent shooting and fishing in the surrounding area, this fine inn is well worth seeking out. When the weather is fine, guests can enjoy their meal on the patio or stroll around the two acres of gardens. In wintertime, the cosy log fires add to the warm and welcoming ambience of this superior inn. Open: Monday to Saturday 11-3 and 6-11; Sunday 12-3 and 7-10.30.

## WOOKEY HOLE  MAP 2 REF G4
1 mile NW of Wells off the A371

The minor roads to the northeast of the A371 Wells to Cheddar road ascend into the Mendip Hills, an area of rolling limestone upland which is popular with walkers, cavers and motorised sightseers. **Wookey Hole**, one of the best known visitor attractions in this Area of Outstanding Natural Beauty, lies on its southeastern edge, two miles to the northwest of Wells. Throughout the centuries, the carboniferous limestone core of the hills has been gradually dissolved by the small amount of carbonic acid in rainwater, an effect which has turned cracks into fissures, fissures into underground rivers and, on rare occasions, underground rivers into immense subterranean caverns such as these.

During the Palaeolithic and subsequent eras, Wookey Hole was lived in by wild animals such as lions, bears and woolly mammoths. Evidence of their occupation is supported by the large cache of prehistoric mammals' bones which was discovered in a recess known as the **Hyena's Den**, many of them showing the animals' teeth marks. There is also evidence of human occupation during the Iron Age. In total, there are over 25 caverns, although only the largest half dozen are open to visitors. The **Great Cave** contains a rock formation known as the Witch of Wookey which casts a ghostly shadow and is associated with gruesome legends of child-eating.

The river emerging from Wookey Hole, the Axe, has been harnessed to provide power for industrial use since the 15th century. The present building on the site was originally constructed in the early-1600s as a paper mill.

## EBBOR GORGE
Map 2 ref G4

3 miles NW of Wells off the A371

The National Trust-owned Ebbor Gorge lies about a mile to the northwest of Wookey Hole. A national nature reserve managed by English Nature, this dramatic landscape offers two scenic walks, the shorter of which takes around thirty minutes to complete and is suitable for wheelchair users accompanied by a strong pusher. The longer walks takes around an hour and a half and involves a certain amount of rock scrambling. The route climbs through woodland inhabited by badger and sparrowhawk, and passes close to caves which are home to greater and lesser horseshoe bats. From the top, buzzards can often be seen wheeling on the thermals above the gorge.

## PRIDDY
Map 2 ref G4

4 miles NW of Wells off the B3135

Lying to the north of the Ebbor Gorge, the isolated settlement of Priddy is the highest village in Somerset. Once more important than it is today, its sizable part 13th century church contains some interesting architectural oddities. The curious thatched structure on the green is a carefully-stacked pile of wooden hurdles. At one time, these were used to construct makeshift pens for Priddy's annual sheep fair, a colourful event which still takes place on the Wednesday closest to August 21. An impressive prehistoric site lies within a mile of the village to the northeast. Thought to be Bronze Age or earlier, **Priddy Circles** are composed of a series of raised banks surrounded by ditches. The nearby tumuli are known as the **Priddy Nine Barrows**.

## WESTBURY-SUB-MENDIP
Map 2 ref G4

4 miles NW of Wells on the A371

To the northwest of Wells, the A371 Cheddar road runs along the base of the Mendip escarpment, through an area which is renowned for its strawberries and soft fruit. Here, the landscape is scattered with attractive Mendip stone villages, including Westbury-sub-Mendip, Significant archaeologoical discoveries have been made in the Mendips above the village.

**The Old Stores** in Westbury-sub-Mendip, located between the village church and pub, is an impressive yet homely house dating back to the 17th century. As

its name suggest it was once the local shop, which has been tastefully converted to provide bed and breakfast accommodation. At the adjacent cottage, known as "The Apple House", self-catering accommodation is available. The furnishings and decor throughout offer a very high standard of comfort and quality. In the main house there are three attractive and

**The Old Stores, Westbury-Sub-Mendip, nr Wells, Somerset BA5 1HA Tel: 01749 870817 Fax: 01749 870980 email: MOGLIN980@aol.com**

very comfortable guest bedrooms. The guests' lounge is a spacious and comfortable room, with an open fire and diversions such as television, radio, books and games. The traditional English breakfast is hearty and delicious, complete with treats such as fresh strawberries in season. Local activities in the area include caving, horse riding, golf, bird-watching, cycling, dry skiing, long-distance walks and shorter rambles. Owner Malcolm Mogford has written a book of local walks which start and finish at the garden gate. He and his wife Linda are friendly and welcoming hosts, who are happy to help guests plan their days if requested. "The Apple House" is a cosy cottage that sleeps two people in traditional country cottage-style comfort. In either the B&B or the cottage, guests are ensured a relaxing and restful retreat, though still near Wells, Cheddar, Bath and the many other attractions of this part of Somerset.

WOOKEY                                                          MAP 2 REF G4
3 miles NW of Wells off the A371

Half a mile east of the village of Wookey, Henley Mill is a handsome private garden with adjacent nursery, **Mill Cottage Plants**, which is open on Wednesdays in spring and summer. This lovely country garden boasts herbaceous borders, old roses and a formal kitchen garden. The River Axe runs through the property, with steep banks and open bridges. While this makes the gardens very attractive, it also makes them unsuitable for small children. Owner Sally Gregson is a professionally trained horticulturist; with the help of her husband Peter she offers visitors guided tours and, from the nursery a vast range of plants. In

August Sally holds Propagation Workshops and in October they host a series of workshops on "Gardening from Scratch". Sally is also available to visit gardening clubs and local WI groups to give illustrated talks. The nursery rears a wide selection of cottage garden perennials, ferns, ornamental grasses and unusual Hydrangeas. Visitors are advised to ring before visiting if they would like a particular plant. There is also a mail-order service available during the winter. Open (in 2000): Wednesdays 10-6 from 1st March to 27th September. At other times, as for example to see the Hellebores before March, please ring for an appointment.

**Mill Cottage Plants, The Mill, Henley Lane, Wookey, Somerset BA5 1AP Tel: 01749 676966**

## EASTON
MAP 2 REF G4
4 miles NW of Wells off the A371

**The Easton Inn** in the quiet hamlet of Easton is worth seeking out. This excellent inn is open daily from midday-3 pm and 5-11; in summer from midday-11pm. It is located just a mile from Wookey Hole. Central for Wells,

**The Easton Inn, Sladebrook Road, Easton, Wells, Somerset BA5 1DU
Tel/Fax: 01749 870220**

Bath, Glastonbury and Cheddar, this fine inn is comfortable and welcoming. The pub is certainly not without character and charm; the stylish, modern interior, open-plan around the bar and separate dining room with a light and airy feel that is markedly different from the more usual low ceilings and dark wood of older establishments. Fully refurbished in 1999, the inn offers the finest in modern comforts. The atmosphere is relaxed and informal. There are always at least two real ales on tap; more in season, as well as a good complement of wines, spirits, lager and ciders. Richard Hughes, formerly from the award-winning Nantyffin pub in Crickhowell, brings a wealth of experience and great flair to his menu. The food changes regularly, to make the most of seasonal favourites. Everything from traditional pub food to sophisticated choices such as guinea fowl, spicy crab cakes, mixed Mediterranean vegetable kebab, grilled lemon sole, fillet steak and oven-baked chicken breast stuffed with red peppers offer something to please every palate. The lunchtime sandwich, baguette and filled ciabattas menu is also a very popular choice. Everything is freshly prepared. The superb home-made desserts are well worth leaving room for. The annual Burns' Night is one highlight of the inn's calendar, which boasts several special evenings of fine food and drink. To the rear of the inn there is an attractive patio and new beer garden commanding wonderful views over the Mendip Hills - just the place to enjoy a relaxing drink or excellent meal on fine days.

## WEDMORE
MAP 2 REF F4

9 miles W of Wells on the B3139

A pleasant drive to the west of Wells follows the old turnpike road across the low moors, now the B3139, to Wedmore, the ancient capital of the Somerset marshes. In 878 AD, King Alfred brought the newly-baptised Danish King Guthrum to this remote village to sign the Peace of Wedmore, a treaty which left Wessex in Alfred's hands and ceded East Anglia, East Mercia and the Kingdom of York to the Danes. Wedmore's largely Perpendicular parish church of St Mary has a spectacular Norman south doorway which is thought to have been carved by the craftsmen who built Wells cathedral. The main street, the Borough, is lined with fine stone buildings, including the George, a lovely old coaching inn, and Church Street is a delightful thoroughfare with a grassy bank on one side which curves upward towards the church.

## BURTLE
MAP 2 REF F4

10 miles W of Wells off the B3151

The **Tom Mogg Inn** in Burtle - located between Bridgwater and Street off the A39 near Erdington - is a lively and welcoming public house and inn set in the heart of rural Somerset - your hosts are Janet and Steve Gilbert and family. Originally called The Railway Inn, Tom Mogg was the last signalman and porter at Edington Junction, situated just 75 yds away. This distinguished pub has a large L-shaped open-plan bar area with comfortable seating and a large open log fire. There's also a separate bar and games room, suitable for families with young children. The large restaurants have a relaxed and cosy ambience. Renowned with locals and visitors alike, the menu offers a great selection of traditional favourites such as steaks, pies, chicken, fish and gammon dishes, together with a good range of vegetarian choices and lighter

**Tom Mogg Inn, Station Road, Burtle, Somerset TA7 8NU Tel: 01278 723399 Fax: 01278 722724 email: tommogg@telinco.co.uk**

snacks, all expertly prepared and presented, providing superb value for money. The pub hosts a range of exciting events throughout the year, such as murder mystery nights. Accommodation is available in the form of six spacious and lovely en suite guest bedrooms (doubles, twins and family room), furnished and decorated with great style and taste. The inn also boasts a superb beer garden with an old willow tree as a centrepiece and lots of seating. The inn is a real ale pub with at least four local and guest beers always on tap.

## CHEDDAR

A spectacular ravine, the **Cheddar Gorge,** carries the B3371 southwestwards towards the Somerset Levels. One of the most famous and often-visited natural attractions in Britain, it is characterised by towering cliffs of weathered limestone and precariously-rooted bands of undergrowth. As well as being known for its gorge, the sprawling village of Cheddar is internationally-renowned for its caves and, of course, its cheese. Although much embellished by modern tourist paraphernalia, its two main show caverns, **Gough's Cave** and **Cox's Cave,** are worth seeing for their sheer scale and spectacular calcite formations. An almost complete skeleton dubbed "Cheddar Man" was discovered in Gough's Cave in 1903. This can now be seen in a nearby museum along with further evidence of human occupation of the caves, including flint and bone tools dating from the last Ice Age and artefacts from the Iron Age and the Romano-British period. Starting from a little lower down the hill, the 322 steps of **Jacob's Ladder** lead up the side of the gorge to the site of **Pavey's Lookout Tower,** a novel vantage point which offers a spectacular view of the surrounding landscape. An unusual market cross stands at the centre of the old part of Cheddar village. Really two crosses in one, a hexagonal superstructure was added to the original 15th-century preaching cross around a century later.

**The Gardener's Arms** is a welcoming traditional 16th-century country inn. Believed to be the oldest drinking house in Cheddar, it is situated to the north of town, not far from the famous Cheddar Gorge yet well away from the busy tourist trail. The interior is warm and attractive; its walls adorned with photo-

**The Gardener's Arms, Silver Street, Cheddar, Somerset  BS27 3LE**
**Tel: 01934 742235**

graphs of Old Cheddar. The garden is cool and lush, just the place to enjoy a relaxing drink on a summer's day. The pub's innovative menu makes best use of the freshest local ingredients, with all snacks and meals cooked to order. The bar has enticing nooks and crannies and an open fire at each end. The emphasis is on superb food and good beer, with a selection of real ales, wines, lager and spirits, making the inn popular with locals and visitors alike. Huw and Jo Davies take justified pride in providing a warm welcome and excellent standard of service at this superior pub.

The term Cheddar cheese refers to a recipe which was developed in the mid 19th century by Joseph Harding, a farmer and pioneer food scientist from near Bath who made the first scientific investigation into cheese-making.  As the name refers to a recipe and not the place, the cheese can be made anywhere in the world; however, North Somerset is dotted with cheese manufacturers of various sizes, from single farmhouses to large-scale dairies.  A number of these supplement their income by offering guided tours, craft demonstrations and catering facilities.

**The Cheddar Gorge Cheese Company** is several attractions in one. This marvellous craft village includes a wealth of craftspeople at work, and of course the chance to sample and see the famous cheese being made, from rich unpasteurised local milk to muslin-wrapped and rinded 56-pound rounds. Visitors can enjoy fudge-making demonstrations, try their hand at a potter's wheel, see lace-makers and candle-makers plying their traditional trades, and much more. The only cheesemaking company actually located in Cheddar, it is home to the true character of this renowned cheese, the result of several unique factors, the most important being the milk source and the traditional methods involved in making and maturing it. Local legend has it that cheese was discovered accidentally when a milkmaid who left a pail of milk in the nearby Cheddar Caves

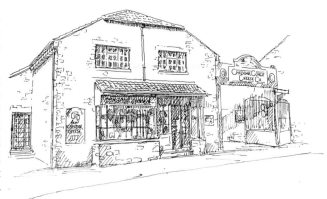

**The Cheddar Gorge Cheese Company, The Cliffs, Cheddar, Somerset BS27 3QA**
**Tel: 01934 742810 Fax: 01934 741020**

later returned to find that the milk had turned into a new and very tasty substance. The Cheddar Valley has been home to cheesemaking for over 800 years; some of the village caves would be used to store cheese, because of their constant cool temperature. Cheddar Gorge Cheese has found its way to many of the country's finest hotels and shops, such as Harrod's, The Savoy Hotel, and even Buckingham Palace itself. The shop within this superb craft village sells a variety of strength and flavours of the cheese, ranging from medium cheeses matured for about six months to vintage cheeses matured for 14 months. Natural flavours include cider, chive, garlic, mustard, white wine, port, chilli, smoked applewood, herb and ginger. And to top it off, why not stop for a break and some refreshments in the lovely Conservatory Restaurant? Open daily from mid-March until the end of October.

**Market Cross Hotel** in Cheddar is a gracious and elegant hotel offering a range of services and superb accommodation. Taking its name from the town cross, literally just a step away, this delightful hotel makes a perfect base for exploring the area. Owner Anne Fieldhouse is a friendly and conscientious host, who makes every effort to ensure that all her guests have a relaxing and comfortable stay. The standard of service is beyond reproach, and the staff always pleasant and helpful. The six well-appointed and charming guest bedrooms offer every amenity, combining exquisite style and a lovely decor with all the modern touches today's guests have come to expect. There are also self-catering

apartments available, just adjacent to the hotel in the 'Sungate' Georgian house. Dating back to the 1800s, this distinguished Regency hotel occupies a quiet spot yet is within easy walking distance of the town centre. The welcoming visitors' lounge is furnished in period style,

**Market Cross Hotel, Church Street, Cheddar, Somerset BS27 3RA Tel: 01934 742264 Fax: 01934 741411**

and features a licenced bar for guests. The traditional English breakfast is hearty and delicious; evening meals are also available by arrangement. The food is of an excellent standard and the evening menu boasts a wide variety of traditional and more innovative dishes; light refreshments can always be obtained until 10 p.m. Attention to detail and a variety of extras such as morning newspapers, and packed lunches at just £4.50 per person (to be ordered the night before), are just part of the excellent range of services offered at this superior hotel. Local sights and attractions within easy walking distance include adventure caving, a leisure centre, riding stables, and of course Cheddar Gorge and the picturesque Mendip Hills. Just a little further afield, other facilities include golf, fishing and an artificial ski slope.

## AROUND CHEDDAR

### CHARTERHOUSE
MAP 2 REF G3
3 miles NE of Cheddar off the B3371

Rising in places to over 1000 feet above sea level, the Mendips form a landscape unlike any other in Somerset. Although it is hard to imagine today, these picturesque uplands were once an important lead and silver mining district, with the last mine at Priddy remaining open until 1908. Mendip lead-mining activity was centred around Charterhouse, a remote village lying four miles to the northwest of Priddy. The settlement takes its name from a Carthusian monastery, **Witham Priory**, which owned one of the four Mendip mining sectors, or Liberties. The area had been known for its mineral deposits since the Iron Age; indeed, such was its importance that the Romans declared its mines state property within six years of their arrival in Britain. Under Roman influence, silver and lead ingots, or pigs, were exported to France and Rome, and the settlement grew into a sizable town with its own fort and amphitheatre, the remains of which can be still be made out today. Improved technology in later centuries allowed for the reworking of the original seams, and the area is now littered with abandoned mine buildings and smelting houses.

## BURRINGTON COMBE
3 miles N of Cheddar on the B3134

MAP 2 REF G3

A path from Charterhouse church leads up onto the 1,067-foot **Black Down**, the highest point in the Mendips. To the northwest, the B3134 descends through Burrington Combe, a deep cleft which is said to have provided the Reverend Augustus Toplady with the inspiration for his hymn, *Rock Of Ages*.

## AXBRIDGE
1 mile W of Cheddar off the A371

MAP 2 REF F3

To the west of Cheddar, the A371 skirts around Cheddar's curious circular reservoir before passing to the north of Axbridge, an ancient small town with a delightful centre which is well worth making a detour to visit. During the Saxon era, Axbridge was a fortified market town which had its own mint, then in the late medieval period, it was a prosperous wool centre which made its living processing Mendip fleeces into woven cloth. Although nothing whatsoever to do with the monarch in question, **King John's Hunting Lodge** in the Square is an exceptional example of a half-timbered merchant's house dating from around 1500. (Its name is a reminder that the Mendip hills were once a royal hunting forest.) Now owned by the National Trust, it was extensively restored in the 1970s and now houses an excellent local museum.

The magnificent parish **Church of St John** also overlooks the Square. A fine example of Somerset Perpendicular, it stands at the top of an impressive flight of steps and contains some exceptional monumental brasses and stained glass. The centre of Axbridge contains an unusual number of handsome Georgian shops and town houses and is best explored on foot.

## LOWER WEARE
2 miles W of Cheddar on the A38

MAP 2 REF F3

Lower Weare is situated two miles to the west of Axbridge near the point the A38 crosses the River Axe. A minor road to the northwest of here leads to the hamlet of Webbington Loxton, home of an interesting visitor attraction, the **Wheel-wright's Working Museum** and **Gypsy Folklore Collection**.

## CHAPEL ALLERTON                                        MAP 2 REF F4
4 miles SW of Cheddar off the B3151

The only complete windmill in Somerset can be found in the lanes to the south of Lower Weare in the village of Chapel Allerton. Well worth making a detour to visit, this superb 18th century stonebuilt **Tower Mill** still was once the principal flour mill for the locality.

## BRENT KNOLL                                            MAP 2 REF F3
9 miles SW of Cheddar off the B3140

The A38 to the southwest of Lower Weare leads over the M5 motorway to Brent Knoll, a conspicuous landmark which can be seen from as far away as South Wales. Before the Somerset Levels were drained, this isolated hill would almost certainly have been an island. Like many other natural features of the landscape which appear out of place, there are stories that the knoll owes its existence to the Devil. It rises to 445 feet and is topped by the remains of an Iron Age hillfort. Several centuries later, its southern slope is reputed to have been the site of a battle against the Danes which was fought and won by King Alfred. The summit, which can be reached by way of footpaths starting near the churches at East Brent and Brent Knoll, affords a spectacular view over the surrounding landscape. The churches at **East Brent** and Brent Knoll are both exceptional. The former has a superb 17th century plasterwork ceiling and a collection of carved bench ends which incorporate the abbot of Glastonbury's coat of arms and initials. The latter also contains an interesting series of bench ends which tell the cryptic story of how the local parishioners, who are represented by geese and other creatures, won a dispute with the 15th-century abbot, who is represented by a fox.

## BERROW                                                 MAP 2 REF E3
10 miles SW of Cheddar on the B3140

The B3140 to the west of Brent Knoll leads to Berrow and Brean, two ancient settlements on the Bristol Channel coast which have been overwhelmed by 20th-century development. Each has a part 13th century church which looks somewhat out of place amongst the surrounding seaside attractions.

## BREAN                                                  MAP 2 REF E3
10 miles W of Cheddar off the A370

The magnificent sandy beach to the north of Berrow is over five miles long. At its northern margin, it is sheltered by the 320 foot high **Brean Down**, an imposing remnant of the Mendip hills which projects into the Bristol Channel. (Another fragment can be seen in the shape of the offshore island, **Steep Holm**). The remains of an Iron Age coastal fort and a Roman temple have been discovered on the Down which is now a designated nature reserve under the protection of the National Trust. The Victorian fortifications at the western tip were partially demolished in 1900 when a soldier accidentally fired his rifle into the ammunition store. With one of the widest tidal ranges in Europe, the currents around the headland can be dramatic and very dangerous. Brean Down is also home to the fascinating **Brean Down Bird Garden**.

**The Old Rectory Motel** is a delightful place to stay while exploring this region of Somerset. There are eight en suite guest bedrooms, including family rooms, and one self-catering apartment. Access to five miles of lovely sandy beach is just two minutes' walk from the motel. Fully accessible to people with disabilities, this fine establishment boasts a range of facilitiesdesigned to ensure guests' comfort and enjoyment of their stay. Set in three-quarters of an acre of lush gardens, including a safe play area, paddock and walled garden, this is a very pleasant rural haven for any holiday-maker. The accommodation is spacious and modern. The traditional full English Breakfast is hearty and delicious; evening meals are available by prior arrangement. Facilities

**The Old Rectory Motel, Church Road, Brean, Burnham-on-Sea, Somerset TA8 2SF Tel/Fax: 01278 751447**

nearby include golf, swimming, fishing, horse riding and many good restaurants. The motel makes an ideal base from which to explore local places of interest such as Cheddar Caves, Wookey Hole and Secret World.

## BURNHAM-ON-SEA                                               Map 2 ref E4
10 miles SW of Cheddar on the B3140

Further south, Burnham-on-Sea is a sizable seaside town with a wide sandy beach which at low tide seems to extend for miles. When mineral springs were discovered here in the late 18th century, an attempt was made to reinvent the resort as a spa town to rival Cheltenham and Bath. However, the efficacious effects of its waters were never properly demonstrated and in the end it had to fall back on its beach to attract visitors. The west tower of the part 14th-century parish church has a worrying lean owing to its sandy foundations. Inside, there is a remarkable Jacobean altarpiece which was originally made for Whitehall Palace; designed by Sir Christopher Wren, the carving has been attributed to Grinling Gibbons. The **Low Lighthouse**, the curious square structure raised above the beach on tall stilts, is perhaps Burnham's most distinctive landmark.

## HIGHBRIDGE

MAP 2 REF E4

10 miles SW of Cheddar on the A38

AdjoiningBurnham-on-Sea to the southeast, the small townof Highbridge was once a busy coastal port at the mouth of the Glastonbury Canal. A couple of noteworthy places of interest lie within easy driving distance of here. The **Secret World** badger and wildlife rescue centre at New Road Farm in East Huntspill offers a wide range of attractions and activities related to the wildlife of the area, including a badger observation set, bee hives and nature trail. It is situated off the B3141.

Another "natural" attraction is **Alstone Wildlife Park** between Highbridge and Bridgwater on the A38. Here, visitors can meet Theadore the friendly camel, some Kune Kune "Kiwi" pigs, Pippa the roe deer, Zac and Zebedee the llamas, and see ponies, emu, goats, eagle owls and more. This small non-commercial family-run park is well worth a visit, and includes a delightful picnic area.

## WEST HUNTSPILL

MAP 2 REF E4

10 miles SW of Cheddar off the A38

**The Sundowner Hotel** in West Huntspill is a distinctive and welcoming hotel. Dating back to the 1770s, with 19th- and mid-20th-century extensions, this spacious and airy establishment has been a hotel since the early 1960s. This distinguished establishment is owned and personally run by Mike and Elaine Runnalls, ably assisted by their daughter Marina, who offer all their guests genuine hospitality and conscientious service. An air of peace and informality reigns here, as the hotel manages to combine the best of traditional and modern features to ensure guests' every comfort. There are eight lovely en suite guest bedrooms (doubles and twins), providing guests with every modern amenity amid comfortable surroundings. The furniture and fittings are of the highest quality, offering the best standard of comfort. There is an attractive and welcoming residents' lounge and bar. The light and airy open-plan restaurant, open to residents and non-residents alike, offers ideal surroundings for enjoying dishes from the extensive and varied menu, which offers a range of tempting delights, from hearty lunchtime favourites such as cottage pie and sirloin steaks to choices from the à la carte menu, which include appetisers like *moules marinière* and

The Sundowner Hotel, 74 Main Road, West Huntspill, nr Highbridge,
Somerset  TA9 3QU Tel: 01278 784766  Fax: 01278 794133
e-mail: runnalls@msn.com

spicy king prawns to main courses of escalope of veal, honey roast duckling, swordfish and stuffed aubergines. On Sundays there's an excellent traditional roast, and after any meal it's worth leaving room for the home-made desserts. All dishes are expertly prepared and presented by the hotel's qualified chef, who has been employed here since 1988 and makes use of the freshest and best quality local ingredients. Facilities nearby include horse riding, golf, walking, birdwatching, coarse and sea fishing, excursions to the coast and all the fine sights and attractions of the region. The hotel also boasts superior conference facilities.

# 5 Southeast Somerset

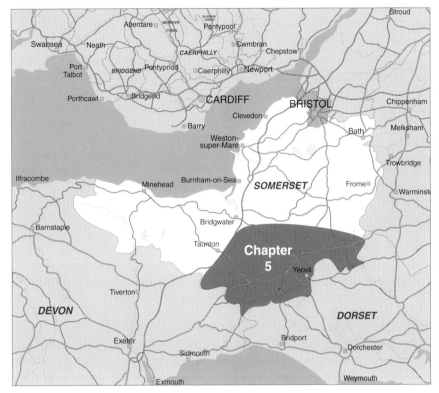

A good place to begin any tour of southeast Somerset is from the **Wellington Monument**, the conspicuous 170 foot obelisk which stands on a spur of the Blackdown Hills overlooking the Vale of Taunton Deane, just off the M5. This striking landmark was constructed in honour of the Duke of Wellington on the estate bought for him by the nation following his victory at the Battle of Waterloo. (Despite his adopted title, the Duke had no connections with the locality and is known to have visited the estate only once in 30 years.)

The monument's foundation stone was laid in 1817 following a wave of enthusiastic public support. However, the necessary funds to complete the project did not materialise and a number of radical economies had to be introduced. These included the redesigning of the structure to give it three sides instead of four and the cancelling of an ostentatious cast iron statue of the Duke which had been proposed for the top. As it was, the modified triangular pinnacle remained unfinished until 1854, two years after Wellington's death. Visitors can still make the formidable 235-step climb to the top where they are rewarded with spectacular views across lowland Somerset to Exmoor and the Mendips.

## ILMINSTER

The old ecclesiastical and agricultural centre of Ilminster lies near the junction of the A358 and A303. Meaning "minster on the River Isle", the settlement takes its name from the church which was founded here by the Saxon King Ine in the 8th century. The borough was recorded in the Domesday Book as having a market and three mills, and during the medieval era it grew to become a thriving wool and lace-making town. This period of prosperity is reflected in the town's unusually large parish church, a magnificent 15th century minster whose massive multi-pinnacled tower is modelled on Wells cathedral. Thanks to a Georgian restoration the interior is surprisingly plain; however, it does contain a number of interesting tombs and monumental brasses. A stroll around the old part of Ilminster reveals a number of lovely old buildings, many of which are constructed of golden Ham stone. These include the chantry house, the old grammar school and the colonnaded market house.

**Dillington House**, on the outskirts of Ilminster, is a handsome part-Tudor mansion which is the former home of the Speke family. In the time of James II, John Speke was an officer in the Duke of Monmouth's ill-fated rebel army which landed at Lyme Regis in 1685. However, following its disastrous defeat at Sedgemoor, he was forced to flee abroad, leaving his brother, George, who had done no more than shake the Duke's hand, to face the wrath of Judge Jeffreys. The infamous Hanging Judge sentenced poor George to death, justifying his decision with the words, "His family owes a life and he shall die for his brother." Dillington House is currently leased to Somerset County Council and functions as an adult education centre.

## AROUND ILMINSTER

BLAGDON HILL                                                    MAP 2 REF E6
8 miles W of Ilminster off the B3170

**The White Lion** is situated on the Honiton Road from Taunton, halfway up the Blackdown Hill range. Built in 1605, it takes its name from a nickname for Arthur Wellesley, 1st Duke of Wellington, who was known as the White Lion after his success at Waterloo. The name also commemorates the workmen who brought thousands of tons of stone up the hill for the building of the Welling-

**The White Lion, Blagdon Hill, Taunton, Somerset TA3 7SG Tel: 01823 421296**

ton monument. The open-plan bar area boasts exposed timber ceilings and an old oak settle. Porcelain, brasses and copper implements adorn the pub, along with old prints and bric a brac of bygone years. Owners Becky and Brian Hinton are friendly and welcoming hosts.

Becky trained in hotel catering, and brings the benefit of her experience to the fine menus of bar meals and main courses, offering guests a choice of traditional favourites such as steaks, breast of chicken and vegetarian options. Meals can be taken in the bar or in the separate non-smoking restaurant. All food is prepared and cooked to order using the freshest local ingredients available.

Travelling northeast, the B3170 leads to **Poundisford Park**, a small H-shaped Tudor mansion standing within a delightful wooded deer park which once belonged to the bishops of Winchester. The house is renowned for its fine plasterwork ceilings and the grounds incorporate a formal garden laid out in the Tudor style. A little further on, the B3170 leads past the superb **Widcombe Wildlife and Country Park**.

## HATCH BEAUCHAMP
Map 2 ref E6
5 miles NW of Ilminster off the A358

One of the finest country houses in the area can be found at Hatch Beauchamp, just off the A358 Ilminster road. Built of attractive honey-coloured limestone in two phases during the second half of the 18th century, **Hatch Court** was designed in impressive Palladian style by the Axbridge architect, Thomas Prowse. Among its finest features are the hall with its cantilevered stone staircase, the curved orangery with its arched floor-to-ceiling windows, and the semicircular china room with its elegant display of rare porcelain and glass. There is also a fine collection of 17th and 18th century English and French furniture, 19th and 20th century paintings, and a small military museum commemorating Britain's last privately-raised regiment, the Princess Patricia's Canadian Light Infantry. The extensively restored grounds incorporate a walled kitchen garden, rose garden, arboretum and deer park.

## WRANTAGE

MAP 2 REF E6

6 miles NW of Ilminster on the A378

Within easy reach of Taunton, Glastonbury, Wells and the many scenic and cultural attractions of the area, **The Canal Inn** in Wrantage is a fine public house offering great food, drink and accommodation. Dating back to the 1700s, the pub's open-plan L-shaped bar area boasts exposed ceiling beams, open fires and a separate res-taurant area to the rear. The restaurant is in fact the oldest part of the original building, with original ceiling tim-bers and a vast timber lintel over the fireplace. Real ales are served, as well as a good range of wines, lagers, spirits and soft drinks. The menu features traditional and international

**The Canal Inn, Wrantage, Taunton,
Somerset TA3 6DF Tel: 01823 480210
e-mail: the-canal-inn@tinyworld.co.uk**

cuisine along with changing daily specials. Dishes such as salmon steak, curries, spinach cannelloni, chicken, beef and gammon offer something to tempt every palate. For owners Jacqueline and John Walbridge, this pub is the fulfilment of a lifelong dream. They bring a wealth of experience and enthusiasm to the enterprise, and are welcoming hosts.

## ILTON

MAP 2 REF F6

2 miles N of Ilminster off the A303/A358

The charming village of Ilton is mentioned in the Domesday Book, and retains some delightful old and distinguished buildings.

**The Wyndham Arms** enjoys a long and distinguished history. Dating back to the 16th century, it proudly displays the Wyndham family crest - an influen-tial family in the area from the time of Queen Elizabeth I. The lounge bar is the ideal place to enjoy a relaxing drink and a bar meal, the house speciality being home-made soups and pies. Why not also enjoy a game of table skittles or traditional skittles with the regulars in the locals' bar? The well-stocked bar of this Free House features real ales and guest beers, as well as a fine complement of lagers, wines and spirits. A taste of traditional country fare awaits guests at The Room on the Green Restaurant, a welcoming and inviting place with hand-

The Wyndham Arms, Ilton, nr Ilminster,
Somerset TA19 9EY Tel/Fax: 01460 52164

some wood panelling and traditional furniture. All dishes use only fresh local produce, in a menu that is varied but always impressive, combining classic English favourites with more innovative creations, all home cooked and delicious. The restaurant is open for lunch and evening meals Monday to Saturday, and for lunch on Sunday. Accommodation available.

## SHEPTON BEAUCHAMP                    MAP 2 REF F6
3 miles NE of Ilminster off the A303

The remains of a medieval open strip field system can still be made out from the air at Shepton Beauchamp, a mile to the southeast of Barrington Court, or for some heritage of a different kind it is worth visiting Westport, on the B3168 one and a half miles to the north. This tranquil community is a former inland port which was built at the height of the canal era by the Parrett Navigation Company for exporting wool and stone and importing coal and building materials.

## BARRINGTON                          MAP 2 REF F6
3 miles NE of Ilminster off the B3168

Three miles to the northeast of Ilminster, a lane to the east of the B3168 leads to the beautiful National Trust-owned **Barrington Court**. The house was built in middle of the 16th century from local Ham stone and displays the characteristics of the architectural transformation from Tudor Gothic, with its buttresses and mullioned and transomed windows, to Renaissance, with its twisted finials and chimney stacks. The garden was laid out in the 1920s in a series of themed areas, including the iris garden, lily garden, white garden and fragrant rose garden. The celebrated landscape architect, Gertrude Jekyll, was brought in to advise on the initial planting and layout, and the garden remains the finest example of her work in the Trust's care. There is also an exceptionally attractive one-acre kitchen garden with apple, pear and plum trees trained along the walls which in season produces fruit and vegetables for use in the restaurant. The nearby estate village of Barrington contains some fine old Ham-stone cottages.

## HAMBRIDGE                                                    MAP 2 REF F6
5 miles NE of Ilminster off the B3168

**Brown and Forrest**, Purveyors of the finest smoked Eel and Salmon - so reads the sign marking the entrance to this wonderful traditional smokery. Estab-lished nearly 20 years ago, this professional establishment offers a range of mouth-watering delica-cies including smoked duck breast, ham and cheese, for sale direct to visitors or to be enjoyed in the fine licenced restaurant. There is also a thriving mail order service. Owner Michael Brown still uses traditional continental wood-fired kilns to produce superb results us-ing beech and apple woods for smoking eel, and oak for salmon and trout. Visitors learn about the craft of smoking, and can watch as marinaded eels are loaded into the hot-smoker. As a special serv-ice for anglers, Brown and Forrest offer a unique service: bring them your salmon or trout, and they'll smoke it for you! The informal and charming restaurant on site enjoys a warm and friendly atmosphere;

the menu offers a range of light lunches, morning coffee, puddings and, of course, excellent smoked eel and smoked salmon dishes.

**Brown and Forrest, Bowdens Farm,
Hambridge, nr Curry Rivel,
Langport, Somerset TA10 0BP
Tel: 01458 251520 Fax: 01458 253475**

Open: Monday-Friday 10.00 am - 4.00 pm and Saturdays 10.00 am - 2.00 pm (closed Bank Holidays).

## DRAYTON                                                     MAP 2 REF F6
6 miles NE of Ilminster off the A378

The privately-owned **Midelney Manor** can be found at Drayton. Originally an island manor belonging to the abbots of Muchelney, this handsome 16th to 18th-century manor house has been owned by the Trevilian family since the early 1500s. The estate incorporates a heronry, a series of delightful gardens and woodland walks, and the unique 17th-century Falcons Mews.

## MUCHELNEY

MAP 2 REF F6

6 miles NE of Ilminster off the A372

Muchelney is the location of an impressive part-ruined Benedictine monastery which was founded in Saxon times around 950. During the medieval period, **Muchelney Abbey** grew to emulate its great rival at Glastonbury; however, after the Dissolution of the Monasteries in 1539, the building gradually fell into disrepair and much of its stone was removed to provide building material for the surrounding village. In spite of this, a substantial part of the original structure remains, including the south cloister and abbot's lodge. Now under the custodianship of English Heritage, the abbey is open daily, 10am to 6pm between 1 April and 30 September. An exhibition of pottery by John Leach and furniture by Stuart Interiors can be seen in the abbey grounds.

Muchelney's parish church is worth seeing for its remarkable early 17th-century illuminations on the ceiling of the nave. Opposite stands the **Priest's House**, a late-medieval hall house with large Gothic windows which was originally a residence for priests serving at the church across the road. This has been refurbished by the National Trust.

Coarse fishing, camping and a lovely caravan site are provided at **Thorney Lakes**, a lush and peaceful place one mile from the historic village of Muchelney. Two secluded lakes, each spanning two acres and surrounded by trees, are stocked with a selection of coarse fish including large carp to provide excellent coarse fishing. The farm, covering some 300 acres, rears beef and cereals, and has won conservation awards. The camping/caravan site boasts a modern toilet block and free hot showers, and is suitable for people with disabilities. It can accommodate up to 16 caravans. This peaceful retreat also makes an excellent base for visiting the local attractions and sights in Muchelney and the surrounding area, including Barrington Garden,

**Thorney Lakes and Caravan Site, Thorney Farm, Muchelney, Langport, Somerset TA10 0DW Tel: 01458 250811**

Long Sutton Golf Course and more. This fine location is also a welcome haven for those wishing to rest and relax amid lovely and tranquil surroundings.

## HUISH EPISCOPI
Map 2 ref F5
7 miles NE of Ilminster off the A372

One of the finest examples in the county of a late-medieval "Somerset" tower can be found on the church at Huish Episcopi, an ancient community which almost adjoins Langport to the southeast. At its most impressive in high summer when viewed through the surrounding greenery, this ornate honey-brown structure is adorned with striking tracery, pinnacles and carvings. The church also possesses an elaborate Norman doorway, which shows signs of having been affected by the fire that destroyed much of the earlier building in the 13th century, and a window in the south chapel which was designed by the 19th century Pre-Raphaelite, Edward Burne-Jones.

## LANGPORT
Map 2 ref F5
8 miles NE of Ilminster on the A378

The small former market town of Langport lies three miles along the A378 to the northeast of Curry Rivel. The old part of the town stands on a rise above an ancient fording point on the River Parrett, a short distance downstream from where it is joined by the rivers Isle and Yeo. The **Langport and River Parrett Visitor Centre** provides visitors with an opportunity to learn about life on the Somerset Levels and Moors, with a hands-on "discovery room", cycle hire and more.

Defended by an earthwork rampart during Saxon times, by 930 Langport was an important commercial centre which minted its own coins. The town's surviving east gate incorporates a curious "hanging" chapel which sits above the arch on an upper level. The tower at Huish Episcopi can be seen through its barrel-vaulted gateway. Langport's own parish church is worth a look for its beautiful stained-glass windows and finely-carved 12th-century lintel over the south doorway.

During the 18th and 19th centuries, Langport flourished as a banking centre, and the local independent bank, Stuckey's, became known for their impressive branches, many of which can still be seen in the surrounding towns and villages trading under the banner of NatWest. At the time of its amalgamation in 1909, Stuckey's had more notes in circulation than any other in the country except the Bank of England.

Throughout history, the **Langport Gap** has been the site of a number of important military encounters. Two of the most significant occurred over 1000 years apart: the first involved Geraint, King of the Dumnonii in the 6th century, and the second, the Battle of Langport of July 1645, gave Parliament almost total control of the South West during the English Civil War.

## ALLER MAP 2 REF F5

9 miles NE of Ilminster on the A372

Another historic event occurred in the church at Aller, two miles along the A372 Bridgwater road to the northwest of Langport. It was here in 878 AD that King Alfred converted Guthrum the Dane and his followers to Christianity following a battle on Salisbury Plain. The low wooded rise to the east of Aller is crisscrossed by a network of ancient country lanes. These connect some pleasant hamlets and villages, among them High Ham, the location of the last thatched windmill in England. Dating from 1822 and remaining in use until 1910, the **Stembridge Tower Mill** is now under the ownership of the National Trust.

## SOMERTON MAP 2 REF G5

12 miles NE of Ilminster off the B3153

The B3153 to the east of Langport leads to Somerton, a fine old town which was the capital of Somerset for a time under the West Saxons. The settlement grew up around an important crossroads to the northwest of the church. However, an expansion towards the end of the 13th century altered the original layout and created the present open market place with its distinctive **Market Cross** and town hall, both later additions. Between 1278 and 1371, Somerton became the location of the county gaol and meeting place of the shire courts. It also continued to develop as a market town, a role which is reflected in such delightfully down-to-earth street names as Cow Square and Pig Street (now Broad Street).

**Somerton Market Cross**

Present-day Somerton is filled with handsome old shops, inns and houses, the majority of which are constructed of local bluish lias limestone. The general atmosphere of mature prosperity is enhanced by the presence of a number of striking early buildings. These include the 17th-century **Hext Almshouses** and the part 13th-century church with its magnificent 15th-century tie-beam roof and unusual transeptal south tower.

The words "country house" call to mind gracious rural living amid scenes of rural splendour in relaxed and supremely comfortable surroundings. All this and more comes to life at **The Lynch Country House**, a charming and elegant Grade II listed Bed and Breakfast hotel with five beautiful en suite bedrooms. On the edge of Somerton overlooking a superb countryside landscape including the local wildlife sanctuary, this stylish bucolic retreat dates back to the 18th century and is set amid superb formal and natural gardens, including a lake that is home to black swans, exotic ducks and other fish and fowl. Secluded and tranquil, it is also convenient for exploring Bath, Bristol, Wells and Taunton, all of which are within easy distance.

**The Lynch Country House, Somerton, Somerset TA11 7PD Tel: 01458 272316 Fax: 01458 272590 e-mail: the_lynch@talk21.com**

The furnishings and decor are elegant and in keeping with the grandeur of the house itself. Each bedroom is individually furnished, named and fitted to the highest standards of comfort and quality. The traditional English breakfast is prepared using the freshest local ingredients. There are several excellent places to eat lunch and dinner, some within walking distance.

## CHARD

On the northern approaches to Chard, the A358 Ilminster to Axminster road passes close to two contrasting places of interest. To the west, **Hornsbury Mill** is a 200 year old corn mill which has an impressive working water wheel, and to the east, **Chard Reservoir Nature Reserve** is a conservation area which offers a varied two-mile circular walk through rustling reed beds, broad-leaved woodland and open hay meadows. An important habitat for wildlife, the lake is home to a number of rare bird species, including the kingfisher and great crested grebe.

**The Furnham Inn** on the edge of Chard along the main road to Ilchester is a handsome and traditional public house. Built as an inn in the late 1700s, the building is a Grade II listed structure. Popular with locals and visitors alike, the

**The Furnham Inn, Furnham Road, Chard,
Somerset TA20 1AP Tel: 01460 62415**

atmosphere is relaxed and informal. Owner Helen Webber is the epitome of the welcoming and friendly pub landlady, and has been here at inn since 1981. Experienced, conscientious and helpful, she leads her staff in providing excellent service and real hospitality. Laid out in traditional style with a separate bar and lounge, simple and hearty snacks and meals are on offer, together with a good range of beers, wines and spirits. Outdoors there's a spacious and attractive beer garden and secure play area for children complete with climbing frames and other diversions. Two skittle alleys and darts are also available for guests' pleasure.

Chard is today a pleasant light industrial town whose population of 12,000 has more than doubled since the Second World War. The borough has was established in 1235, and during medieval times it was a prosperous wool centre with its own mayor, or portreeve, and burgesses. However, with the exception of the fine Perpendicular parish church, few buildings date from before 1577, the year of the devastating fire which razed most of the town to the ground. (Perhaps this is how Chard got its name?!) Chard's gradual reconstruction has left it with some fine 16th and 17th century buildings, including the courthouse and old grammar school, and there are also a number of striking Georgian and Victorian structures, most notably the neoclassical town hall of 1835 with its impressive two-tier portico. An unusual round toll house with a conical thatched roof can also be seen on the outskirts of the town.

**Chard and District Museum**

Despite its rapid postwar development, the centre retains a pleasant village-like atmosphere which is particularly apparent around the broad sloping main street. A good way to find out more about the town's eventful past is to visit the award-winning **Chard Museum** in Godworthy House. This impressive local museum is housed in an attractive thatched building at the west end of the High Street.

# AROUND CHARD

WAMBROOK                                                                    MAP 2 REF E7
1 mile W of Chard off the A30

Those with an interest in animal welfare should make a point of visiting the **Ferne Animal Sanctuary at Wambrook**. Situated off the A30 a couple of miles to the west of Chard, this delightful establishment was originally founded in 1939 by the Duchess of Hamilton and Brandon when she lived at Berwick St John near Shaftesbury. Since 1975, it has been located in its present position overlooking the valley of the River Yarty on a 51-acre site which incorporates a nature trail, conservation area, dragonfly pools and picnic areas.

BISHOPSWOOD                                                                 MAP 2 REF E6
4 miles NW of Chard off the A303/B3170

The evocatively-named **Candlelight Inn** is a handsome traditional stonebuilt inn dating back to the 17th century. In the midst of rural Somerset yet within easy reach of Taunton, Chard, Wells, Glastonbury, Bath and Bristol, this traditional country inn has a warm and friendly ambience; the staff are helpful and conscientious, and owners Graham and Karen are welcoming hosts. There's a paddock to the rear, and an attractive tea garden. The River Yarty runs along the bottom of the garden. The open-plan main bar area offers a wealth of exposed beamwork, wall timbers, open fireplace and exposed stonework walls. There's a good selection of beer, wine and spirits. At one end is the lounge-style area

The Candlelight Inn, Bishopswood, Chard,
Somerset TA20 3RS Tel: 01460 234476

for pre/after dinner drinks; at the other is the dining area. The menu features a range of snacks and main courses at both lunchtime and evening, including home-made soup, hearty sandwiches, steaks, cod fillet, pies, pork tenderloin, scampi, lasagne and more, all freshly prepared and cooked to order.

## TATWORTH

MAP 2 REF E7

1 mile SE of Chard off the B3167/B3162

On the edge of Chard, adjacent to Forde Abbey and gardens, **The Poppe Inn** is a delightful thatched public house dating back to 1485. Original features include the exposed beamwork and flagged floors. Owners Sharon and Allan Madgin are hospitable and conscientious hosts. Said to be haunted by the ghost of a nun, who has manifested herself to Allan and the pub's chef several times,

guests can appreciate why she might want to stick around: the ambience, warmth and friendliness of this pub is truly welcoming. Meals are available in the main bar or the separate (no-smoking) restaurant. The menu offers an impressive list of innovative and traditional dishes such as pan-fried lamb's liver, T-bone

**The Poppe Inn, Tatworth, nr Chard, Somerset TA20 2NZ Tel: 01460 220260**

steaks, venison, prawn and smoked salmon tagliatelle and much more, all expertly prepared and presented. There are always three real ales on tap, together with a good selection of lagers, wines and spirits.

Between Tatworth and Forton, east of Forton Lane, lies a meadow watered by springs rising on its borders. This meadow is the last remaining sign of "common" land first enclosed in 1819. Changes in land ownership during the 1820s allowed too many farmers with grazing rights, and the meadow suffered from over-stocking. In 1832 holders of these "rights" met, and so a tradition was born. Calling their meeting "Stowell Court", and auctioned off the meadow for one year, sharing in the proceeds. The auction proceedings were unique: commencing when a tallow candle precisely one inch long was lit, and ending with the last bid before the candle failed! The Stowell Court still meets on the first Tuesday after April 6th every year, and many more customs have been added is over the years. Stowell Mead is now managed as a Site of Special Scientific Interest, as meadow land which is treated with no fertilisers, pesticides or herbicides, and so still home to many plants generally rare in the countryside. There is no right of way through the land, but a seat has been placed just inside the meadow at the Forton Lane end.

## FORDE ABBEY
Map 2 ref F7

3 miles SE of Chard off the B3162/B3167

One of the loveliest country houses in England lies in the lanes four miles southeast of Chard. Set in the beautiful valley of the River Axe, **Forde Abbey** was founded as a Cistercian monastery in the 12th century and took more than four centuries to complete. To prevent its destruction following the Dissolution of the Monasteries in 1539, the abbot offered the property to the crown and it became a private mansion. Today it is the family home of the Ropers and contains an outstanding collection of tapestries, period furniture and paintings. The refectory, dormitory and chapter house survive from the medieval

**Forde Abbey, near Chard, Somerset TA20 4LU**
**Tel: 01460 221290**

monastery, which is surrounded by 30 acres of superbly landscaped grounds encompassing lakes, a bog garden, nursery and walled kitchen garden. The estate is also known for its pedigree herd of cattle and incorporates a pick-your-own fruit farm. The house is open April-October on Sundays, Tuesdays, Wednesdays, Thursdays and Bank Holiday, 1 - 4.30; gardens open daily all year round from 10 a.m.

## DOWLISH WAKE
Map 2 ref F6

3 miles NE of Chard off the B3168

Those with an interest in traditional cider making should make a point of finding **Perry's Cider Mills** at Dowlish Wake, a pleasant community which lies hidden in the lanes to the southeast of Ilminster.

**Perry's Cider Mills**

The village contains some attractive honey-coloured Ham-stone cottages and an imposing parish church which stands on a steep rise a little way from the centre. Inside can be seen the tomb of John Hanning Speke, an intrepid Victorian explorer who journeyed for over 2,500 miles through some of the harshest terrain in Africa to confirm Lake Victoria as the source of the River Nile. Speke returned to England a hero, but tragically, on the very morning he was due to report his findings to the British Geographical Association, he accidentally shot himself while out partridge shooting.

## CRICKET ST THOMAS                                    MAP 2 REF F7
3 miles E of Chard off the A30

The former estate village of Cricket St Thomas lies on the A30, three miles to the east of Chard. This hamlet is home to the **Cricket St Thomas Wildlife and Leisure Park** (formerly the home of one of Britain's least hidden places, Noel Edmonds' **Crinkley Bottom** television theme park). Attractions include a horse stables, children's adventure fort, wildlife world, and a varied assortment of themed crowd pullers designed to bait the very young. Although it may be hard to imagine today, **Cricket House** was once the family home of the great 18th century naval commander, Admiral Sir Alexander Hood, and later of the Bristol chocolate manufacturer, F J Fry. The estate incorporates the tiny church of St Thomas with its impressive monument to Admiral Hood, later Viscount Bridport.

Adjacent to the Wildlife park and close to Forde Abbey, **The Firs** is a modern, spacious and comfortable family home offering superior bed and breakfast accommodation. Set in two acres of pastureland either side of the main house, it has spacious gardens which guests are welcome to explore, and offers easy access to nearby Chard. There is golf and squash within walking distance, and a Leisure Centre with swimming pool at Chard. Exeter is just 35 miles away, Lyme Regis 15 miles away; the towns of Yeovil and Crewkerne are also within easy access. A welcoming and homely atmosphere pervades this charming B&B, which is furnished and decorated to a high standard of comfort and quality. There are three large double guest bedrooms, one en suite and two with private bath. A

**The Firs, Crewkerne Road, Cricket St Thomas, nr Chard,
Somerset TA20 4BU Tel/Fax: 01460 65646/65259**

travel cot and high chair are also available. Owner Sheila Bright is a warm and friendly host. The traditional full English breakfast is hearty and delicious. No smoking.

## HINTON ST GEORGE
MAP 2 REF F6
5 miles NE of Chard off the A356

A lane to the north of Windwhistle Hill leads to the former estate village of Hinton St George, an unspoilt Ham-stone gem which for centuries was owned, and left virtually untouched, by the Poulett family. The Pouletts rebuilt Hinton House shortly after their arrival here in the 15th century, and this structure now forms the core of the present-day mansion. This has now been converted into apartments, although local people say it continues to be haunted by the ghost of a young Poulett woman who died of a broken heart after her father shot dead the man she was planning to elope with.

Several ostentatious monuments to members of the Poulett family can be seen in the superb little 15th century church of St George. With its pinnacled tower and imposing interior, this is perhaps the most outstanding feature of the village. Another noteworthy building is the so-called Priory, a 16th century residence with a 14th century window at its eastern end which is thought to have once belonged to Monkton Farleigh Priory in Wiltshire. It is a tradition for Hinton children to beg candles to put inside their intricately-fashioned turnip and pumpkin lanterns on "Punkie Night", the last Thursday in October. It is thought to be very unlucky to refuse them, as each lantern is said to represent the spirit of a dead person who, unless illuminated, will rise up at Hallowe'en.

## CLAPTON
MAP 2 REF F7
6 miles E of Chard on the B3165

Another delightful landscaped garden can be found beside the B3165, four miles to the east of Forde Abbey. The 10-acre **Clapton Court Gardens** are some of the most varied and interesting in Somerset. Among the many beautiful features are the formal terraces, rose garden, rockery and water garden. The grounds incorporate a large wooded area containing a massive ash tree which, at over 230 years old and 28 foot in girth, is believed to be the oldest and largest in mainland Britain. There is also a fine metasequoia which is already over 80 foot tall, having been planted in 1950 from seed brought back from China.

## MOSTERTON                                    MAP 2 REF F7
7 miles SE of Chard on the A3066

In the village of Mosterton, three miles further east on the A3066 Crewkerne to Bridport road, David, Benjamin and Simon Eeles produce a unique range of handmade stoneware and porcelain at the **Eeles Family Pottery**. At certain times, visitors can view the pots being thrown and decorated before they are taken for firing in the family's three-chambered dragon kiln.

## CREWKERNE                                    MAP 2 REF F7
7 miles E of Chard on the A356

The ancient former market town of Crewkerne lies at the junction of the A30 and A356, three miles to the north of Mosterton. Like Chard and Ilminster, the town developed as a thriving agricultural and market centre during Saxon times and even had its own mint in the decades leading up to the Norman invasion. The magnificent parish **Church of St Bartholomew** was built on the wealth generated by the late-medieval boom in the wool industry. A structure of minster-like proportions, it is one of the grandest of the many fine Perpendicular churches to be found in south Somerset.

Unlike most other towns in Wessex whose textile industries suffered an almost total decline, Crewkerne was rejuvenated in the 18th century when the availability of locally-grown flax led to an expansion in the manufacture of sailcloth and canvas webbing. Among the many thousands of sails to be made here were those for HMS *Victory*, Nelson's flagship at the Battle of Trafalgar. The town's resurgence was further boosted by the development of the London-Exeter coaching route at this time, a factor which led to the rebuilding of old Crewkerne in elegant Georgian style. Many fine town houses and inns from this period can still be seen in the centre, most notably in Church and Abbey streets, now an Area of Outstanding Architectural Interest. Less appealing are the northern and southern outskirts of the town which been given up to large-scale light industrial development.

The A30 to the west of Crewkerne climbs onto the aptly-named **Windwhistle Hill**, a high chalk-topped ridge which enjoys dramatic views southwards to Lyme Bay and northwards across the Somerset Levels to the mountains of South Wales. This is also the location of the impressive Windwhistle golf and country club.

**The River Parrett Trail** passes over the lovely **Haslebury Bridge**, a medieval packhorse bridge, on its way between Bridgwater and Crewkerne. Approximately 50 miles long, the Trail passes through one of Britain's most ecologically sensitive and fragile areas, the Somerset Levels and Moors. Old mills, splendid churches, attractive and interesting villages and towns - and historical sights including Europe's largest Iron Age fort, at Ham Hill in Stoke-sub-Hamdon, up through Langport and beyond. Walkers will also find orchards, peaceful pastureland and traditional industries such as cider making and basket-weaving.

## HASELBURY PLUCKNETT                    Map 2 ref G7
9 miles E of Chard on the A3066

The A30 to the northeast of Crewkerne crosses the upper reaches of the River Parrett before being joined by the A3066 Bridport road. The delightfully-named community of Haselbury Plucknett lies half a mile south of this junction. Another gem of a village, it has a large part-Norman church whose churchyard contains a series of unusual "squeeze stones".

## WEST CHINNOCK                          Map 2 ref F6
9 miles NE of Chard off the A356

**The Muddled Man** public house in West Chinnock, near Crewkerne, is a lively and welcoming place. Dating back to the 1600s, this handsome stonebuilt pub with its humourous and unusual name is pristine and comfortable. Outside there's a spacious lawned and walled beer garden - a secure and relaxing space in which to enjoy a quiet pint or some delicious food. The interior boasts low beamed ceilings, leaded light windows, handsome old stone fireplace and other traditional features. The open-plan bar area encourages the informal and relaxed atmosphere of the place. Mick and Jean Medcalf, ably assisted by their son Gary, are hosts

**The Muddled Man, Lower Street, West Chinnock, Crewkerne, Somerset  TA18 7PT Tel: 01935 881235**

par excellence, amicable and knowledgeable about the sights and attractions of the area. This quintessentially traditional English country pub is a pleasure to pass time in, with its friendly atmosphere and great food and drink. Real ales are on tap, and everything from snacks to three-course roasts available on the menu, all home-cooked and home-prepared.

WEST COKER                                                                 MAP 2 REF G6
11 miles NE of Chard on the A30

The magnificent **Brympton d'Evercy Manor House** lies in the lanes to the north of West Coker, two and a half miles from the centre of Yeovil. Norman in origin but with major 16th and 17th century additions, it has a superb golden Ham-stone south wing which was built in Jacobean times to a design influenced by Inigo Jones. It many fine internal features include the longest straight single-span staircase in Britain and an unusual modern tapestry showing an imaginary bird's eye view of the property in the 18th century. The little estate church of St Andrew boasts a sturdy square bell tower and some fine medieval monuments. When seen from a distance, the mansion, church and nearby dower house make a delightful lakeside grouping. (Open by appointment only by telephoning 01935 862528.)

   **The Castle Inn** in West Coker is a lovely stonebuilt, thatched building dating back to around 1540. It has been carefully tended and looked after over the years, and newly thatched in 1999, so presents a handsome and pristine exterior to the world. It has also had a long and varied history, being in its time a private dwelling and butcher's shop, and now housing a friendly and welcoming public house and restaurant. The interior features inglenook fireplaces at each end of the bar, as well as a central log fire, decorative stained glass and a wealth of other attributes that make it both comfortable and attractive. Real ales, wines, spirits and lagers are available. In the separate large

**The Castle Inn, The High Street, West Coker,
Somerset BA22 9AT Tel/Fax: 01935 862331**

and spacious restaurant, guests can choose from the extensive and varied menu of dishes from 'light bites' such as sandwiches and bar snacks to tempting main courses including steaks, grills, fish and chicken dishes, and vegetarian choices. There are also daily specials. All are expertly prepared and presented. The attractive beer garden and barbecue area is just the place to wile away a lazy summer day.

# YEOVIL

With its 28,000 inhabitants and strategic position at the junction of several main routes, Yeovil is the largest centre of population in south Somerset. A modern light industrial and market town whose best-known employer is Westland Helicopters, it offers a comprehensive range of shopping and recreational facilities. Despite its up-to-date character, Yeovil's origins go back to the time of the ancient Romans. During the Middle Ages, a lively livestock and produce market was established in the town which continues to be held here every Friday.

Yeovil's parish **Church of St John the Baptist** is the only significant medieval structure to survive, most of its other early buildings having been destroyed in a series of town fires in the 17th century. A substantial Ham-stone structure dating from the second half of the 14th century, the church has surprisingly austere exterior given its exceptional number of windows. (Indeed, it has so many that it is sometimes referred to as the "lantern of the West"). Perhaps its finest internal feature is the plain brass lectern which is believed to date from around 1450. One of only five still in existence, it is the only one to be found in a parish church. During the 18th century, Yeovil developed into a flourishing coaching and industrial centre whose output included gloves, leather, sailcloth and cheese. This rapid expansion was enhanced by the arrival of the railway in the mid 19th century, then in the 1890s, James Petter, a local ironmonger and pioneer of the internal combustion engine, founded a business which went on to become one of the largest manufacturers of diesel engines in Britain. Although production was eventually transferred to the Midlands, a subsidiary set up to produce aircraft during the First World War has since evolved into the present-day helicopter plant.

A fascinating museum documenting the social and industrial history of the area from prehistoric and Roman times through to the agricultural and industrial revolutions can be found near the Octagon Theatre in the centre of Yeovil. Situated in Wyndham House in Hendford, the recently-refurbished **Museum of South Somerset** uses a series of imaginative settings to recapture the atmosphere of the times.

Right in the centre of Yeovil, **Mulberry's Bistro** is a friendly and welcoming restaurant. The conservatory, patio, profusion of plants and touches like the musical instruments and other adornments lend a homely and festive air to this

**Mulberry's Bistro, 9 Union Street, Yeovil,
Somerset BA20 1PQ Tel/Fax: 01935 434188
e-mail: mulbistro@aol.com
website: www.yeoviltown.com**

charming eatery. Spacious, airy and light, there are tables indoors and out where guests can enjoy a drink, snack or full meal. The cuisine on offer is international, boasting a range of a la carte and bistro fare, fine wines, morning coffee and more. Relaxing and pleasant, this makes a perfect place to enjoy a quiet meal or just a break from sightseeing around Yeovil. The menu features steaks, scampi, salmon, lamb and other traditional favourites, superbly prepared and beautifully presented. A selection of pasta, chilli, vegetarian and curry dishes add to the many choices faced by diners. This charming restaurant is open Monday to Saturday 10 a.m.-2.30 p.m. lunch and 7-closing (last orders 2.30 p.m. and 10.30 p.m. respectively)

## AROUND YEOVIL

BARWICK                                            MAP 2 REF G6
2 miles S of Yeovil off the A37

Two miles south of Yeovil, a turning to the east off the A37 leads to Barwick Park (pronounced Barrik), an estate dotted with bizarre follies. Arranged at the four points of the compass, the eastern folly known as **"Jack the Treacle Eater"** is composed of a rickety stone arch topped by a curious turreted room. According to local lore, it is named after a foot messenger who ran back and forth to London on a diet of nothing but bread and treacle. The estate also possesses a curious grotto and a handsome church with a Norman font and an unusual 17th century transeptal tower.

## EAST LAMBROOK
MAP 2 REF F6

7 miles NW of Yeovil off the B3165

The charming hamlet of East Lambrook is home of the beautiful **East Lambrook Manor Garden**. The garden was laid out by the writer and horticulturalist, Margery Fish, who lived at the medieval Ham-stone manor from 1937 until her death in 1969. Her exuberant planting and deliberate lack of formality created an atmosphere of romantic tranquillity which is maintained to this day. Now Grade I listed, the story of the genesis of the project is told in her first book, *We Made A Garden*. The National Collection of cranesbill species geraniums is also kept here.

The low-lying land to the north of East Lambrook is crisscrossed by a network of drainage ditches, or rhines (pronounced reens), which eventually flow into the rivers Parrett, Isle and Yeo. Originally cut in the early 1800s, the ditches are often lined with double rows of pollarded willows which have come to characterise this part of Somerset. Despite having to be cleared every few years, the rhines provide a valuable natural habitat for a wide variety of bird, animal and plantlife.

## MARTOCK
MAP 2 REF F6

5 miles NW of Yeovil on the B3165

The attractive small town of Martock lies on the northern side of the busy A303. Surrounded by fertile arable land, the district has long been renowned for its prosperous land-owning farmers. The community's long-established affluence is reflected in its impressive part 13th-century parish church. A former abbey church which once belonged to the monks of Mont St Michel in Normandy, it boasts one of the finest tie-beams roofs in Somerset, almost every part of which is covered in beautiful carvings.

The old part of Martock contains an unusual number of fine buildings. The National Trust-owned **Treasurer's House** is situated opposite the church. Recently refurbished, this handsome part 13th-century residence incorporates a medieval great hall and cross wing, and a kitchen annexe which was added around 1500. The nearby **Old Court House** is a former parish building which served the locality for 200 years as a grammar school, and to the west, Martock's 17th-century Manor House is the former home of Edward Parker, the man who exposed the Gunpowder Plot after Guy Fawkes had warned him against attending Parliament on the fateful night.

**The Somerset Guild of Craftsmen Gallery** at Yandles of Martock contains a fascinating range of work made by the county's craftspeople. Items on display include musical instruments, spinning wheels, turned wood, furniture, ceramics, textiles, silver and metalwork.

On the edge of Martock, **Madey Mills** is a welcoming traditional farmhouse offering bed and breakfast accommodation. Once two working mills set amid

this farm environment, home to 300 years of dairy farming, it is reached via a private lane. Amid the rural tranquillity, the accommodation is warm and friendly, furnished in an informal and very comfortable style. There are three guest bedrooms (two singles, and a double). Owner Diana Clarke is a conscientious and accessible host, happy to help ensure that her guests have a relaxing and enjoyable stay. Guests are free to roam the many open spaces, where free-ranging farm animals abound. The farmhouse breakfast is hearty and quite ruinous to the waistline, but guests will find it impossible to resist. This charming establishment makes an ideal base from which to explore the nearby National Trust attractions and all the other sights in the area.

**Madey Mills, East Street, Martock, Somerset TA12 6NN Tel: 01935 823268**

## LITTLE NORTON
MAP 2 REF G6
5 miles W of Yeovil off the A303

This peaceful hamlet nestles beneath Ham Hill in a particularly idyllic part of south Somerset. Set in six acres of superb gardens and grounds, **Little Norton Mill** is a rural haven offering all the peace, tranquillity and comfort guests could ask for. The grounds include a fully restored 18th-century water mill and mill pond, stocked with pet aylesbury ducks and visiting wild ducks. Here in this

**Little Norton Mill, Little Norton, Norton Sub Hamdon, Somerset TA14 6TE Tel/Fax: 01935 881337**

marvellous setting, guests will find eight comfortable self-catering cottages and apartments. All properties are furnished and decorated to a high standard of comfort and quality, and all boast fully equipped kitchens and other amenities. Four of the cottages have two bedrooms, spacious open-plan living/dining rooms and superb views of the mill pond and/or garden. Two cottages have bedrooms with lovely four-poster beds. The original mill barn has been tastefully converted to form four cosy one-bedroom apartments, each of which sleep two. Two are on the ground floor. There are many opportunities for excellent walking and cycling in the area, and guests are also welcome to use the tennis court nearby by arrangement.

## MONTACUTE                                          MAP 2 REF G6
4 miles W of Yeovil off the A3088

The superb National Trust-owned **Montacute House** lies on the southern side of the A3088 Martock road, four miles to the west of the town centre. The present mansion was built in the 1580s by Edward Phelips, Queen Elizabeth's Master of the Rolls, and is considered a masterpiece of Renaissance architecture. Constructed of golden Ham stone to an H-shaped design, it is adorned with characteristic open parapets, fluted columns, twisted pinnacles, oriel windows and carved statues. The long gallery, one the grandest of its kind in Britain, houses a fine collection of Tudor and Jacobean portraits which are on permanent loan from London's National Portrait Gallery. Other noteworthy features include the stone and stained-glass screen in the great hall, and Lord Curzon's bath, an Edwardian addition which is concealed in a bedroom cupboard. An established story tells of how Curzon, a senior Tory politician, waited at Montacute in 1923 for news that he was to be called to form a new government. The call never came.

Montacute House stands within a magnificent landscaped park which incorporates a walled formal garden, a fig walk, an orangery, and a cedar lawn formerly known as "Pig's Wheaties's Orchard".

Five hundred years before the present Elizabethan house was built, a controversial castle was constructed on the nearby hill by William the Conqueror's half-brother, Robert, Count of Mortain. The Saxons were angered by his choice of site, for they believed it to be a holy place where King Alfred had buried a fragment of Christ's cross. In 1068, they rose up and attacked the castle in one of the many unsuccessful piecemeal revolts against the Norman occupation. Ironically, a subsequent Count of Mortain was found guilty of treason and forced into founding, and then donating all his lands to, a Cluniac priory on the site now occupied by Montacute village. The castle has long since disappeared, as has the monastery, with the exception of its fine 16th century gatehouse, now converted to a private house, and a nearby stone dovecot.

Montacute is also home to the **TV & Radio Memorabilia Museum**, hosting a fine collection of vintage radios and radiograms, wireless receivers and early television sets, as well as a variety of books, magazines, annuals and other memorabilia of the great (and sometimes kitsch) world of early TV and radio. The museum also has information on some pleasant local walks in the area.

## CHILTHORNE DOMER
MAP 2 REF G6

3 miles NW of Yeovil off the A37/A3088

**The Halfway House Inn** is distinctive and attractive brickbuilt inn offering food, drink and accommodation together with genuinely warm hospitality. Owner Paul Rowsell and his courteous, welcoming staff make every effort to ensure guests have a pleasant time. The accommodation comprises 12 en suite guest bedrooms (a mixture of singles, twins and doubles), all fitted with all the

modern amenities guests have come to expect. Modern, light and airy, they are comfortable, clean and welcoming. Guests can partake of the delicious and filling full English Breakfast. In the inn's fine dining area, the varied menu offers a range of tempting meals from bar snacks to à la carte beef, fish and chicken

**The Halfway House Inn, Chilthorne Domer, nr Yeovil, Somerset BA22 8RE  Tel: 01935 840350**

dishes, as well as vegetarian choices and, of course, full Sunday luncheon. To the rear of the inn there's a fine beer garden, children's play area and site for up to 20 caravans.

## STOKE-SUB-HAMDON
MAP 2 REF G6

6 miles NW of Yeovil on the A303

The lanes to the west of Montacute lead to Stoke-sub-Hamdon, another attractive village whose eastern part contains a fine part-Norman church and whose western part contains the remains of a late-medieval priory. The latter was built in the 14th and 15th centuries for the priests of the now-demolished chantry chapel of St Nicholas. The remains, which include an impressive great hall, are now under the ownership of the National Trust.

To the south of the village lies the 400 foot **Ham Hill** (or Hamdon Hill), the source of the beautiful honey-coloured building stone of which so many of the surrounding villages are constructed. This solitary limestone outcrop rises abruptly from the Somerset plain providing breathtaking views of the surrounding countryside. A substantial hill fort was sited here during the Iron Age which was subsequently overrun by the ancient Romans. The new occupants built their own fortification here to guard the Fosse Way and its important intersection with the road between Dorchester and the Bristol Channel at nearby Ilchester.

The Romans discovered that Ham Hill's soft even-grained limestone made a flexible and highly attractive building material which was ideal for constructing villas and temples. Later, the Saxons and then the Normans came to share this high opinion of Ham stone, and by the time quarrying reached its height in the 17th century, a sizable settlement had grown up within the boundaries of the old Iron Age fort of which only a solitary inn remains today. A war memorial to 44 local men who died in the First World War stands at the summit of the hill which has now been designated a country park. The combination of the view, the old earthwork ramparts, and maze of overgrown quarry workings make this an outstanding picnic and recreation area.

## TINTINHULL
Map 2 ref G6

5 miles NW of Yeovil off the A303

Another enchanting National Trust property, **Tintinhull House Garden**, lies in a tranquil position between the A3088, A37 and A303, a couple of miles to the northeast of Ham Hill. Laid out in the early 20th century, the garden is divided by walls and hedges into a series of distinctive areas, each with its own planting theme. These include a pool garden with a delightful lily- and iris-filled pond, a kitchen garden, and a sunken garden which is cleverly designed to give the impression it has many different levels.

The garden is set in the grounds of Tintinhull House, an early 17th-century manor farm to which a spectacular west front was added around 1700. Sadly not open to the public, the house overlooks an attractive triangular green which forms the nucleus of the sprawling village of Tintinhull. A number of other interesting buildings can be seen here, including Tintinhull Court, a part-medieval rectory which was remodelled in the 17th and 18th centuries, the Dower House, which was built by the Napper family in 1687, and St Margaret's parish church, a rare example in Somerset of a rectangular single-cell church.

## ILCHESTER
Map 2 ref G6

6 miles NW of Yeovil off the B3151

Ilchester is a pleasant small town which, like Somerton, is a former county town. In Roman times, the settlement stood at the point where the north-south route between Dorchester and the Bristol Channel crossed the Fosse Way. However, it was during the 13th century that the town reached its peak as a centre of administration, agriculture and learning. Ilchester rose to become the county town of Somerset and three substantial gaols were built here, one of which remained in use until the 1840s. Another indication of its former status, a 13th-century mace thought to be the oldest staff of office in England, has been transferred from the town hall to the County Museum at Taunton Castle.

Roger Bacon, the celebrated scholar, monk and scientist, was born in Ilchester around 1214. He went on to predict the invention of the aeroplane, telescope and steam engine, and was eventually confined for his outspoken ideas. No doubt he would be quietly satisfied by the existence of the aircraft museum at nearby Yeovilton if he were alive today. Today, the town is bypassed by the A303 east-west trunk route and most of the worries of the outside world. The tiny **Ilchester Museum** can be found in the centre of town by the Market Cross. The museum tells the story of Ilchester from pre-Roman times to the 20th century. Exhibits include a Roman coffin and skeleton, and a series of displays describing Ilchester's past as a country town.

## KINGSDON                                                MAP 2 REF G5
7 miles NW of Yeovil off the B3151

The B3151 to the northwest of Yeovil leads to the village of Kingsdon, a mile to the east of which lies the delightful National Trust-owned country house and garden of **Lytes Cary**. This late-medieval manor house was built by succeeding generations of the Lyte family, the best-known member of which is Henry Lyte, the Elizabethan horticulturalist who translated Dodoen's Cruydeboeck from the Dutch to create the celebrated work of reference known as Lyte's Herbal. Dedicated to the Queen, it went on to be reprinted several times as an interest in physic gardening began to develop. The present garden is an enchanting combination of formality and eccentricity: there is an open lawn lined with magnificent yew topiary, an orchard filled with quince, pear and apple trees, and a network of enclosed paths which every now and then reveal a view of the house, a lily-pond or a classical statue. The house was built over a long period and incorporates a 14th-century chapel, a 15th-century hall and a 16th-century great chamber.

## YEOVILTON                                               MAP 2 REF G6
6 miles N of Yeovil off the B3151

One of the world's leading aviation museums is situated on the B3151 three miles to the east of Ilchester. The **Fleet Air Arm Museum** at Yeovilton contains a unique collection of over 80 aircraft, around half of which are on permanent display. There is also an impressive series of exhibits illustrating the history of naval aviation from 1910 to the present day. Special displays include those on World Wars I and II, kamikaze warfare, the Korean War, the Harrier Jump Jet and Concorde. There is also a helicopter simulator and the "Ultimate Carrier Experience", a large and complex exhibit consisting of a flight deck with steam catapult, deck landing site, and eleven carrier-borne aircraft. In addition, there are displays of weapons, medals and memorabilia which bring to life the exciting world of naval aviation and the people who have been part of it.

## QUEEN CAMEL
Map 2 ref G6

8 miles NE of Yeovil off the A303

**Pound Orchard** is an impressive family home offering bed and breakfast accommodation. Owner Laraine Singleton and her partner David have lived here since 1990. It's a modern brick house situated in a quiet cul-de-sac adjacent to the village church, with spacious grounds opening onto greenfields. The garden is lush and peaceful. Laraine has raised a family and now enjoys welcoming her guests into her home - and this shows in the homely, welcoming atmosphere. There are two handsome guest bedrooms (one

**Pound Orchard, Grace Martins Lane, Queen Camel, Somerset BA22 7NS Tel: 01935 851029**

twin and one double). Both rooms are very spacious, well-furnished and comfortable, with all the amenities guests have come to expect. The modern, cosy lounge is open for guests' use, equipped with plush furnishings, television, video and other diversions; it's the perfect place for relaxing in front of the open fire after a day's sightseeing. This charming B&B is within easy reach of Yeovil, Bath, Bristol and many other local attractions. The traditional Full English Breakfast with all the trimmings is served in the very attractive dining room.

## SPARKFORD
Map 2 ref G5

9 miles NE of Yeovil on the A303

Another interesting museum can be found on the northeastern edge of Sparkford, five miles to the east of Yeovilton. Situated beside the A359 near its junction with the A303, the **Haynes Motor Museum** is a unique collection of over 200 veteran, vintage and classic cars and motorbikes which is thought to be the largest of its kind in the UK. Nearly every exhibit is driven at least once every six months around a specially-constructed one-kilometre demonstration track. Special displays include Jaguars, Minis, Chevrolet Corvettes and red-painted sports cars.

## CADBURY CASTLE
MAP 2 REF H5

12 miles NE of Yeovil off the A303

Halfway between Ilchester and Wincanton, the A303 passes along the northern edge of **Cadbury Castle**, a massive Iron Age hill fort which is also reckoned by some to be the location of King Arthur's legendary Camelot. This ancient hilltop site was occupied for some 5000 years from the middle to the Neolithic period right up to the 13th century. Heavily fortified throughout the Iron Age, the Romans are reputed to have carried out a massacre here around 70 AD to put down a revolt by the ancient Britons. A major archeological excavation in the 1960s uncovered a wealth of Roman and pre-Roman remains on the site. It also confirmed the existence of a substantial fortification dating from around 500 AD, the time when King Arthur would have been spearheading the Celtic-British resistance against the advancing Saxons. If Cadbury Castle had indeed been Arthur's Camelot, it is likely that it would have been a timber fortification and not the turreted stone structure mythologised by the storybooks.

The easily-defended hilltop site was again refortified during the reign of Ethelred the Unready, this time against the Danes. The poorly-advised king also established a mint here around 1000 AD, most of the coinage from which was used to buy off the Norse invaders in an act of appeasement which led to the term Danegeld. As a consequence, most of the surviving coins from the Cadbury mint are now to be found in the museums of Scandinavia.

The mile-long stroll around Cadbury Castle's massive earthwork ramparts demonstrates the site's effectiveness as a defensive position. Thanks to the magnificent view from the top, troop movements to the north and west would have been easily spotted, and the important route into the Heart of England, the Fosse Way, would have been clearly visible five miles away to the northwest.

Another exceptional view of south Somerset can be had from the summit of **Corton Hill**, two miles to the south. The site of an ancient beacon, it can be reached by following Halter Path Lane from the village of Corton Denham.

## WINCANTON
MAP 3 REF H5

14 miles NE of Yeovil on the A303

The old cloth-making centre of Wincanton is an attractive former coaching town lying almost exactly half way between London and the long-established naval base at Plymouth. In the heyday of the horse-drawn carriage, up to twenty coaches a day would stop here. At that time the inns could provide lodging for scores of travellers and stabling for over 250 horses. The old sector stands on a draughty hillside above the River Cale. It still contains a surprising number of fine Georgian buildings, some of which were constructed to replace earlier ones destroyed in a town fire in 1747. Apart from 15th century church tower and south porch,chancel and the medieval carving of St Eligius in the north porch, the parish church is a Victorian rebuild.

Modern Wincanton is a peaceful light industrial town whose best-known attraction is probably its **National Hunt Racecourse**. Horse racing began in the locality in the 18th century and moved to its present site to the north of the town centre in 1927. Regular meetings are held here between October and May, or for golfing enthusiasts, the racecourse incorporates a challenging nine hole pay and play course which is open throughout the year. Also worth visiting is the beautiful Hadspen House Garden, which is situated beside the A371 Shepton Mallet road, four miles to the northwest of Wincanton.

## TEMPLECOMBE                                        MAP 3 REF H6
5 miles S of Wincanton on the A357

To the east of Corton Hill, the unusual **Gartell Light Railway** runs through the beautiful swathe of countryside known as Blackmore Vale. Situated near the village of Templecombe, this rare 2 foot gauge line currently runs for almost a mile along the trackbed of the much-loved Somerset and Dorset Railway which was closed over thirty years ago. Trains run every fifteen minutes from Common Lane station, which also has a visitor centre, refreshment room and shop. The nearby **Templecombe Railway Museum** houses a fascinating display of artefacts, photographs and models which tell the story of nearby Templecombe station, once a busy junction where some 130 railwaymen were employed. Telephone 01963 370752 for information on open days.

## HENSTRIDGE                                         MAP 3 REF H6
6 miles S of Wincanton off the A30

**Toomer Farm** occupies an idyllic rural setting within 5 acres of grounds including walled gardens, lawns and orchard areas, dovecote and carp ponds, amid some 500 acres of working dairy and arable farmland. A family-run farm for the past 50 years, the traditional stonebuilt farmhouse dates back to the 1600s. Here, guests are welcome to enjoy superb bed and breakfast accommodation. There are three guest bedrooms (one twin, one double, one family room). These

**Toomer Farm, Henstridge, Templecombe, Somerset BA8 0PH Tel/Fax: 01963 250237**

rooms are unusually spacious, almost the size of apartments, and furnished to a high standard of taste and comfort. All the peace and beauty of the countryside can be found here. An atmosphere of tranquillity pervades this lovely house. Within easy reach of Sherbourne, Wincanton and other local sights and attractions, this charming establishment straddling the Dorset/Somerset border (which runs through the farm), offering a truly and welcome retreat. The excellent country-style breakfast comes with all the trimmings.

## BRUTON
### Map 3 ref H5
5 miles N of Wincanton on the A359

The remarkably well-preserved former clothing and ecclesiastical centre of Bruton is more a small town than a village. A priory was established here in the 11th century on the south side of the River Brue. The former priory **Church of St Mary** is a fine Perpendicular structure with a soaring 100 foot west tower. It also has a rare secondary tower which was built over the north porch in the late 14th century. The church interior is unusually light and spacious, and contains a number of memorials to the Berkeley family, the local lords of the manor who also owned the land on which London's Berkeley Square now stands.

A walk around the streets of Bruton reveals some interesting historic features. The curious square structure across the river from the church is the **Patwell Pump**, a communal parish water pump which remained in use until the early 20th century, and a little further downstream, a 15th century arched packhorse bridge can be seen near the site of the famous part 16th century King's School. Perhaps Bruton's most distinctive building, **The Dovecote**, can be seen on the crest of a hill to the south of here. Built in the 15th century, it is thought to have doubled as a watch tower and is now under the custodianship of the National Trust.

Among the many fine buildings to be seen in Bruton High Street are the Pharmacy, with its elegant 18th century facade, and the intriguingly-named **Sexey's Hospital**, a 17th century almshouse which was founded by Elizabeth I's auditor, Hugh Sexey.

## CASTLE CARY
### Map 3 ref H5
4 miles NW of Wincanton off the A371

The lovely little town of Castle Cary lies to the west of the A371. Once the site of an impressive Norman castle, this has all but disappeared and today, the town has the atmosphere of mature rural calm. The streets contain a number of exceptional old buildings, including the handsome 18th-century post office and distinctive beehive-shaped lock-up gaol which dates from the 1770s. The **Castle Cary District Museum** occupies the splendid Market House in the centre of the town. Largely constructed in 1855, the building incorporates a magnificent 17th-century colonnade. The rectory at Ansford, on the northern edge of Castle

Cary, is the former home of the 18th-century diarist, James Woodforde, whose life seemed to have revolved around the consumption of lavish meals.

## STOURHEAD
MAP 3 REF I5

6 miles NE of Wincanton off the B3092

For those keen to explore this beautiful part of Somerset on foot, the **Leland Trail** long-distance footpath starts at King Alfred's Tower on the glorious National Trust-owned **Stourhead Estate**, six miles to the east of Bruton. The 25-mile trail passes through the wooded hills and valleys of Camelot country and takes in Bruton, Castle Cary, Cadbury Castle and Tintinhull on its way to Ham Hill. A further long-distance footpath, the **Liberty Trail**, then continues southwestwards through the Ham-stone country of south Somerset and finally passes out of the county near **Forde Abbey**.

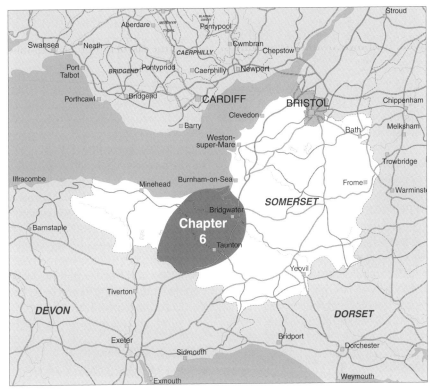

© MAPS IN MINUTES ™ (1998)

# BRIDGWATER

The ancient inland port and industrial town of Bridgwater stands at the lowest medieval bridging point on the River Parrett. Despite having been fortified since before the Norman invasion, the settlement remained little more than a village until an international trade in wool, wheat and other agricultural produce began to develop in the late Middle Ages. During this period, Bridgwater grew to become the most important town on the coast between Bristol and Barnstaple, and the fifth-busiest port in Britain. The largely 14th century parish **Church of St Mary**, with its disproportionately large spire, is the only building to survive from this medieval era of prosperity, the castle having been dismantled after the English Civil War, and the 13th-century Franciscan friary and St John's hospital having long since disappeared. The oldest and most interesting part of the town lies between **King Street** and the West Quay, an area whose layout is medieval, but whose buildings are amongst the finest examples of Georgian domestic architecture in Somerset.

Prior to the construction of a canal dock a short distance downstream early in the 19th century, ships used to tie up on both riverbanks below Bridgwater's medieval three-arched bridge. The last remnant of the castle, **The Water Gate**, can still be seen here on the West Quay, along with a number of fine Georgian residences, the most notable of which, the Lions, was built in 1725.

After a long period of decline brought about by a long-running war with the nation's continental trading partners, Bridgwater underwent something of an industrial renaissance during the first half of the 19th century. The manufacture of Bridgwater glass, which had begun the previous century, continued to expand, and a canal terminus, complete with docks, warehouses, brickworks and retractable railway bridge, was built between 1837 and 1841 a few hundred yards north of the old centre. Finally closed in 1970, the site has been restored and is now a fascinating piece of industrial archeology which is well worth seeing. Bridgwater's manufacturers have long since relocated to the outskirts of town. The most evident of these, a cellophane factory, makes its presence known to residents and visitors alike by its distinctive airborne aroma.

The interior of the parish church is worth seeing for its painting of the *Descent from the Cross* by an unknown Italian artist, and for the fine Jacobean screen which extends across a side chapel. It was from the church tower that the Duke of Monmouth is reputed to have spotted the approaching army of James II the day before the Battle of Sedgemoor. This supposed advantage gave him the inspiration to launch the surprise attack which eventually led to his disastrous defeat in July 1685.

A bronze statue of Bridgwater's most famous son, Robert Blake, can be seen at the top of Fore Street. This celebrated military leader was born in 1598 in the house which now accommodates **Bridgwater's Town Museum**. When in his forties, Blake became an important officer in Cromwell's army and twice defended Taunton against overwhelming Royalist odds, then at the age of fifty, he was given command of the British navy and went on to win a number of important battles against the Dutch and Spanish, so restoring the nation's naval supremacy in Europe. The museum contains a three-dimensional model of the Battle of Santa Cruz, one of his most famous victories, along with a collection of his personal effects.

There is also a similar diorama of the Battle of Sedgemoor and a large collection of locally-discovered artefacts dating from the Neolithic period to the Second World War. Also well worth seeing is Bridgwater's spectacular annual carnival which is held in the town on the first Thursday in November.

# BRIDGWATER TO THE QUANTOCK HILLS

CANNINGTON MAP 2 REF E4
2 miles NW of Bridgwater off the A39

The **Heritage Gardens at Cannington College** contain an impressive collection of rare and exotic plants, a selection of which are for sale in the specialist plant centre.

The **Friendly Spirit** lives up to its name, offering an ideal base for exploring the Quantock Hills, Somerset Levels and the coast. This handsome and welcoming traditional inn is located near the village green and brook, and dates back to the 13th century. The name of this charming inn in fact derives from the amicable resident ghost, said to be that of Maude de Merriett, who lived during the days of King John. Her ghost is said to manifest in the upper rooms to this day. The public and lounge bars are handsomely furnished and comfortable. The dining room is gracious and attractive. The menu offers a wide range of home-cooked meals, from sandwiches to steaks and a good range of daily specials. This fine inn also boasts 10 superb letting bedrooms, offering simple and comfortable lodging for overnight or longer stays. Nearby facilities include golf, cycle hire, archery and horse riding.

**The Friendly Spirit, Brook Street, Cannington, Somerset TA5 2HP Tel: 01278 652215**

DURLEIGH MAP 2 REF E5
2 miles W of Bridgwater off the A39

At Durleigh, in the lanes two miles to the west of Bridgwater, **West Bower Farm** is an extraordinary building which incorporates a twin-turreted medieval gatehouse. The nearby reservoir, which offers good freshwater fishing, is fed by the Bridgwater and Taunton Canal.

## ENMORE
MAP 2 REF E5
4 miles SW of Bridgwater off the A39

Continuing westwards to the village of Enmore, the small redbrick country mansion of **Barford Park** can be found on the road to Four Forks. This delightfully-proportioned Queen Anne house is set in extensive grounds incorporating a walled flower garden, a water garden, an archery glade and a large area of broad-leafed woodland. The interior contains some exceptional examples of Queen Anne furniture and is still in daily family use. (Open by appointment only; telephone 01278 671269.)

To the west of Enmore, the ground rises into the Quantock Hills, an "Area of Outstanding Natural Beauty" which stretches from Kingston St Mary in the south to Quantoxhead on the Bristol Channel coast. Rising to a highest point of 1260ft at Wills Neck near Crowcombe, this delightful area of open heath and scattered woodland supports one of the country's last remaining herds of wild red deer. The exposed hilltops are littered with Neolithic and Bronze Age remains, including around a hundred burial mounds, many of which now resemble simple piles of stones. The richer soil to the south sustains arable farms and pockets of dense woodland. This varied landscape, several tracts of which are owned by the National Trust, offers some excellent opportunities for walking and riding.

## NORTH PETHERTON
MAP 2 REF E5
5 miles SW of Bridgwater off the A38

Set amid 260 acres of countryside, surrounded by pastureland, **Lower Clavelshay Farm** is a peaceful haven of rural tranquillity. A traditional stone and slate building dating back to the 17th century, this charming and welcoming farmhouse offers superb bed and breakfast accommodation. The wealth of original features include beamed ceilings, stone fireplaces and a real log fire in the attractive guests' lounge/

**Lower Clavelshay Farm, North Petherton, nr Bridgwater, Somerset  TA6 6PJ  Tel: 01278 662347**

dining room. The three roomy guest bedrooms (two doubles, one family) are homely and comfortable. Ideally situated for exploring the Quantock Hills, Exmoor National Park or the spectacular North Devon coast, this makes an ideal base. The farm is a haven for wildlife: buzzards, badgers, foxes, deer and birds can be seen, and guests are free to roam this working dairy farm, to see cows being milked, help to feed the pigs or collect the fresh eggs. A cosy family ambience pervades this relaxing rural B&B. Breakfast is a delicious and hearty affair; evening meals are available by arrangement.

## BROOMFIELD
Map 2 ref E5

5 miles SW of Bridgwater off the A38

One of the loveliest areas in the southern Quantocks can be found in the lanes to the south of Enmore around the village of Broomfield. This is the location of **Fyne Court**, the headquarters of the Somerset Trust for Nature Conservation. Leased to the organisation by the National Trust, the 26-acre grounds are a designated nature reserve which incorporates a walled garden, two ponds, a lake and a small arboretum. The main house was built in the 17th century by the Crosse family but was largely destroyed by fire in the 1890s. The only parts to survive were the library and music room, and these have now been converted into an impressive interpretation centre and eating place.

The most renowned occupant of Fyne Court, Andrew Crosse, was an early 19th century scientist who was a pioneer in the field of electrical energy. Known locally as "the thunder and lightning man", one of his lightning conductors can still be seen on an oak tree in the grounds. Rumour has it that during one of his experiments, Crosse created tiny live insects, a claim which helped inspire Mary Shelley to write her Gothic horror story, Frankenstein, in 1818.

## OVER STOWEY
Map 2 ref D4

6 miles W of Bridgwater off the A390

A lane to the south of Nether Stowey rises up towards Over Stowey, the starting point of the Forestry Commission's **Quantock Forest Trail**. This pleasant three-mile walk is lined with specially-planted native and imported trees, most of which have been introduced since World War II. To the northwest of Nether Stowey, **Dodington Hall** is a small privately-owned manor house which is only open to visitors for a few days each year. A Tudor gem set in attractive semi-formal gardens, its great hall features a splendid oak roof and a carved stone fireplace.

## NETHER STOWEY
Map 2 ref D4

6 miles NW of Bridgwater on the A39

Around the turn of the 19th century, the beautiful upland landscape to the west of Bridgwater became a favourite retreat for novelists and poets of the Romantic movement. Nether Stowey is a peaceful village on the northwestern edge of the **Quantocks** which thankfully is now bypassed by the main A39 Bridgwater to Minehead road. In 1797, a local tanner, Tom Poole, lent a cottage at the end of his garden to his friend, Samuel Taylor Coleridge, who stayed there for three years with his wife and child. During this time he wrote "The Rime Of The Ancient Mariner" and sections of "Christabel and Frost At Midnight".

Coleridge was visited on a number of occasions by such literary luminaries of the day as William Wordsworth and Charles Lamb in a colourful invasion which is claimed to have led the locals to believe they were harbouring a den of French spies. **Coleridge's Cottage** is now owned by the National Trust and is open to visitors - please check with the Tourist Information Centre at Bridgwater for details on opening days and times. Coleridge and his friends are rumoured to have drunk at the 400 year-old Castle of Comfort Inn at nearby Dodington.

In Norman times, Nether Stowey was the site of an early motte and bailey castle, the foundations of which can still be seen on the hill to the west of the present-day centre. A substantial manor house, **Stowey Court**, stands at the opposite end of the village. This was begun by Lord Audley in 1497 shortly before he joined a protest against Henry VII's taxation policy. Sadly, he wasn't able to see the project through to completion as he was executed soon after. The clock tower in the centre of Nether Stowey was erected in 1897 to replace a medieval market cross, a reminder that this was once a small market town.

## STOGURSEY
6 miles NW of Bridgwater off the A39

MAP 2 REF D4

The ancient village of Stogursey lies midway between Nether Stowey and the Bristol Channel. In the 13th century, this was the lair of the renegade lord, Fulke de Breaute, who along with a band of ruthless followers, terrorised the surrounding population until he was hunted down and brought to justice. The remains of his castle can still be made out near the village.

## COMBWICH
4 miles NW of Bridgwater off the A39

MAP 2 REF E4

**The Old Ship Inn** is a handsome and welcoming public house, built in the 18th century as a traditional Somerset long house. The open plan long bar, low ceilings and exposed beamwork add to the cosy ambience. A number of original features enhance the decor and atmosphere, as do the decorative brick bar with brass rail and wealth of prints and old photographs adorning the walls. Diana Harris prepares and plans the extensive and varied menus, which offer delicious home-cooked and home-prepared dishes made with the freshest local ingredients. Fish, meat and game dishes are plentiful; there are also imaginative vegetarian options and tempting daily specials. Situated on the edge of the village near the River Parrett, the pub marks the end of the 50-mile Parrett Trail, a rural walk

The Old Ship Inn, Combwich, nr Bridgwater, Somerset  TA5 2QT
Tel: 01278 652348

which spans two counties. A relaxing and friendly retreat, it is the perfect place to enjoy a drink and meal or snack amid convivial surroundings.

## HINKLEY POINT
7 miles NW of Bridgwater on the coast

Map 2 ref E4

The **Hinkley Point Visitor Centre** offers a range of exciting exhibitions outlining the natural history of the Earth, energy needs and how the adjacent power stations work, turning the energy in uranium into electricity. Visitors can arrange to tour either Hinkley A or Hinkley B power station. Times of these tours

Hinkley Point A & B Power Stations, nr Bridgwater, Somerset  TA5 1UD
Tel: 01278 654700  e-mail: j.c.lucas1@ne.british-energy.com

vary throughout the year - please ring for details. The environment around the power stations teems with wildlife; the **Hinkley Point Nature Trail** highlights a wide diversity of habitats and many species of birds, wild flowers, glow worms and more. The trail includes an early Bronze Age burial mound, known locally as **Pixie's Mound**, dating back to 1500 BC and excavated in 1906. A programme of special events, including a bat evening, fungus foray and nocturnal safari, takes place throughout the year. Other facilities include a picnic and play area, retail outlet and café. Open: Monday - Friday, 10 a.m. - 4 p.m.; please ring for details of weekend and holiday opening times. Admission: free.

HOLFORD                                                         MAP 2 REF D4

8 miles W of Bridgwater on the A39

Continuing westwards, the A39 connects a number of charming rural settlements, many of which provide access to the wooded combes and bracken-covered hillsides of the Quantocks. A track from the village of Holford leads up to a large Iron Age hill fortification known as **Dowsborough Fort**. A little further west, two of the most dramatic viewpoints in the Quantocks, **Beacon Hill** and **Bicknoller Hill**, lie on National Trust-owned land overlooking the Bristol Channel and the Vale of Taunton Deane. On the latter can be seen an Iron Age livestock enclosure known as **Trendle Ring**, now an ancient monument.

    **The Plough Inn** in Holford offers great food, good drinking and comfortable accommodation. Owners Mac Cockburn and her son Steve offer a warm welcome to all their guests. Guests of all ages and from all walks of life enjoy the friendly and homely surroundings. The ground floor has two bars, where many guests choose to sample the delights of the varied menu. Home-made soups, sandwiches, bar snacks, pies, curries, beef and chicken dishes and steaks are just some of the tempting options available. A traditional and cosy atmosphere pervades this excellent establishment. Attractive prints and photographs adorn the walls. A good range of ales,

**The Plough Inn, Holford, nr Bridgwater, Somerset TA5 1RY Tel/Fax: 01278 741232**

lagers, wines and spirits are available here. There are three attractive and very comfortable en suite guest bedrooms, equipped with every amenity guests have come to expect, as well as further accommodation in the bunkhouse to the rear of the main house. Dating back to the 1600s, this handsome stonebuilt house has a lovely garden to the rear and ample car parking facilities. The bunkhouse accommodation sleeps up to 12 people, and is particularly suitable for walking or cycling groups and families. Guests are welcome to breakfast in the dining room.

## KILVE
Map 2 ref D4

9 miles NW of Bridgwater on the A39

At Kilve there is a delightful little church with a squat medieval-looking tower. This is thought to date from the 17th century as prior to 1636, the church bells were housed in a wooden structure in the churchyard. The nearby ruins are the remains of a medieval chantry, or college of priests, whose chapel stood to the north of the present church.

A track beyond the churchyard leads down to a boulder-strewn beach, an agreeable place despite its reputation as a favoured haunt of glats, conger eels up to ten feet in length which are known to lie in wait among the rocks near the shore. Once known as "St Keyna's serpents", local people used to search for them using trained "fish dogs".

**The Hood Arms** in Kilve is an attractive and welcoming 17th-century traditional coaching inn and restaurant. It occupies a wonderful coastal location near all the beauty of Exmoor. It sits amid half an acre of gardens, with play area and patio area - a natural suntrap in summer. The interior features two main bars set end to end. Comfortably furnished in traditional style, guests can enjoy a fine

**The Hood Arms, Kilve, nr Bridgwater, Somerset TA5 1EA**
Tel: 01278 741210 Fax: 01278 741477

range of real ales, excellent wines, and a good complement of spirits, lagers, cider and more. The superior menu is extensive and varied, offering everything from lunchtime snacks such as home-made soups and pies to evening meals of hearty steaks, salmon, venison, duck and many other tempting dishes, together with a good variety of daily specials. Accommodation is available in one of five en suite double bedrooms. There's also a self-catering apartment and two charming and comfortable holiday cottages, adjacent to the pub. 'Chough Cottage has a twin and a single bedroom; 'Anchor Cottage' has a twin and a double. Each of the cottages is available for weekend breaks or longer periods during winter months.

**Chantry Cottage** near Kilve Beach is a beautiful stonebuilt and spacious house dating back to the 1200s, rebuilt after fire in the 17th century. The strikingly beautiful ivy-covered shell of the old chantry itself adjoins the house. Occupying a natural setting amid a country garden with flower beds, shrubs and grassland all around, it is a welcoming and bucolic retreat. The interior boasts a warm and traditional farmhouse style with guests' lounge and breakfast room -

**Chantry Cottage and Tea Gardens, Sea Lane, Kilve, nr Bridgwater, Somerset TA5 1EG Tel: 01278 741457
e-mail: jacqui@thechantry.freeserve.co.uk**

adorned with photographs old and new of horse-racing history - and two very comfortable and welcoming guest bedrooms. The traditional English Breakfast is hearty and delicious. At the Chantry Tea Gardens, morning coffee, lunches, afternoon teas, home-made cakes and ice-cream are the tempting offerings here, available all year round. Owners Jacqui and Nick Dawe are friendly and accommodating hosts who make every effort to ensure that their guests have a relaxing and very enjoyable stay.

## WEST QUANTOXHEAD
MAP 2 REF D4

10 miles NW of Bridgwater on the A39

Little remains of the village of West Quantoxhead, or **St Audrie's**, following an extensive redevelopment in the mid 19th century. Its principal features are a Victorian mansion, now occupied by a religous sect, a handsome neo-Gothic church, and a series of unusual gates, fences and walls which create an impression of organised rural respectability.

## EAST QUANTOXHEAD
MAP 2 REF D4

11 miles W of Bridgwater off the A39

From Kilve, a pleasant walk to the northwest leads to East Quantoxhead, a picturesque village containing a delightful assortment of thatched cottages, a mill with a millpond, and a handsome old manor house, **Court House**, which stands within a beautiful garden on a rise overlooking the sea. The owner's family bloodline can be traced back to the time of the Domesday Book. In the 13th century, the manor passed by marriage to the Luttrells, the subsequent owners of Dunster Castle, and in the 16th and 17th centuries the present house was constructed by successive generations of the same family. The church beside the house is a fine example of a late medieval estate church. Inside, there is some fine Renaissance woodwork, an imposing chest tomb commemorating two 16th century members of the Luttrell family, and a rare 14th century rood screen, one of only a handful in Somerset.

# TAUNTON

Taunton, the county town of Somerset, has only been its sole centre of administration since 1936, previous county towns having been Ilchester and Somerton. The settlement was founded as a military camp by the Saxon King Ine in the 8th century, and by Norman times it had grown to have its own Augustinian monastery, minster and castle. An extensive structure whose purpose has always been more administrative than military, the castle was nevertheless the focus of two important sieges during the English Civil War. A few years later, over 150 followers of the Duke of Monmouth were sentenced to death here by the infamous Judge Jeffreys during the Bloody Autumn Assizes which followed the Pitchfork Rebellion of 1685. Even now, the judge's ghost is said to haunt the castle grounds on September nights.

Taunton's historic Castle is home to the **Somerset County Museum**, a highly informative and impressive museum containing a large and important collection of exhibits on the archaeology, natural and human history of the county. There is a wealth of exceptional material evidence in the archaeology galleries, illuminating prehistoric and Roman Somerset. Notable items include wooden trackways from the Somerset Levels, the Low Ham Roman mosaic and a Bronze Age shield, recently found at South Cadbury. In the museum's Great Hall there are displays of wonderful decorative art, glassware, costumes, ceramics, silver, toys and dolls. Among the fossils and minerals are the skeleton of a sea serpent or ichthyosaur. Local industrial history is explored as well, in a series of exhibits tracing the development of steam, oil and electric engines. The museum also boasts a special display chronicling the colourful history of the Somerset Light Infantry, as part of the Somerset Military Museum within the castle. Visitors can also explore the medieval almshouse in the castle courtyard. Throughout the year there are changing programmes of special events and exhibitions, such as concerts, book sales, living history weekends, Roman cookery and much more. Exhibitions past and present for children and adults have included 'Cycling in Somerset', seascapes and marine

**Somerset County Museum, Castle Green, Taunton TA1 4AA**
Tel: 01823 320201  Fax: 01823 320229
e-mail: county-museums@somerset.gov.uk
website: www.somerset.gov.uk/museums

paintings, and prints and drawings by local artists. Activities for school groups and opportunities to learn and have access to the many fine exhibitions enable all visitors to benefit from a visit to this excellent museum. The museum shop sells a good selection of fun and fascinating books, games and craftware. Open: 1st April - end October Tuesday to Saturday and Bank Holiday Mondays 10-5; 1st November - March Tuesday to Saturday 10-3. Admission to the museum also allows the visitor entrance to the Somerset Rural Life Museum in Glastonbury.

Somerset's famous County Cricket Ground occupies part of the old priory grounds which once stretched down to the river. A section of the old monastic gatehouse known as the Priory Barn can still be seen beside the cricket ground. Now restored, this medieval stone building now houses the fascinating **Somerset County Cricket Museum**.

**Somerset County Cricket Museum**

In common with many other towns and villages in the West Country, Taunton was a thriving wool, cloth-making, and later silk, centre during the late middle ages. The profits earned by the medieval clothiers went to build not one, but two huge churches: St James' and St Mary's. Both have soaring Perpendicular towers, which have since been rebuilt, and imposing interiors; the former contains a striking carved stone font and the latter an elegant painted roof adorned with angels. The town centre is scattered with other fine buildings, most notably the timber-framed Tudor House in Fore Street and the 17th-century almshouses.

Present-day Taunton continues to be an important commercial centre with a lively weekly market and a thriving light industrial sector which benefits from some excellent transport links with the rest of the country. Other visitor attractions include **Vivary Park**, with its ponds, gardens and jogging trail, and the impressive Brewhouse Theatre and Arts Centre.

At the heart of Taunton visitors will find the **Brewhouse Theatre and Arts Centre**, and at the heart of the Brewhouse visitors will find Overtures Restaurant and Servery Bar. Diners can enjoy a wide range of dishes from morning coffee and lunch to afternoon tea and pre-show suppers. The restaurant offers

**Brewhouse Theatre and Arts Centre, Coal Orchard, Taunton, Somerset TA1 1JL Tel: 01823 274608**

a variety of delicious meals with vegetarian options. There is always a choice selection of puddings and desserts. Energy and enthusiasm for the arts are the bywords here as a presenting house for musical and theatrical events. The Brewhouse offers a full complement of drama, music, dance, comedy and children's shows, and has become a lively hub as a meeting place. The Brewhouse Theatre and Arts Centre boasts impressive meeting facilities, including the 350-seat auditorium, purpose-built conference rooms and workshop studio.

A pleasant walk follows the towpath of the **Bridgwater and Taunton Canal**, a 14-mile inland waterway which was constructed in the 1820s and fully reopened in the summer of 1994 following decades of neglect and a 20 year programme of restoration. A relative latecomer when it first opened in 1827, the canal was constructed as part of an ambitious scheme to create a freight route between Exeter and Bristol which avoided the treacherous journey around the Cornish peninsula. For many years, the canal was the principal means of importing coal and iron from South Wales to the towns of inland Somerset, and of exporting wool and agricultural produce to the urban centres of Britain.

The towpath winds its way through some of the most attractive countryside in the Somerset Levels, and the restored locks, swing bridges, engine houses and rare paddle-gearing equipment add interest to the walk. The canal also offers a variety of recreational facilities, including boating, fishing, canoeing and bird watching, and passes close to some attractive villages. At North Newton, there is a small country manor, **Maunsel House**, which is occasionally open to visitors, and at Creech St Michael, there is a part 13th-century church which is worth seeing for its fine wagon roof. At the canal's southern end, boats have access to the River Tone via **Firepool Lock** in the heart of Taunton.

# AROUND TAUNTON

ASHE                                                                                          MAP 2 REF E6
2 miles E of Taunton off the A358/A303

Equidistant from the north coast, south coast and the wilds of Exmoor, with the Quantock Hills and Somerset Levels nearby and within an hour's drive of the exciting centres of Bristol, Exeter, Bath and Wells, **Ashe Farm Caravan and Camping Site** makes an ideal base from which to explore the county. This quiet, informal family-run site occupies six acres and is part of a working farm in the Vale of Taunton. Set in two sheltered meadows commanding fine views of the hills, it boasts an atmosphere of seclusion and tranquillity. Amenities include electrical hook-ups, small toilet unit in each field, large block with showers, hot water and razor points, a laundry with tumble dryer and a pay phone. Two fully equipped holiday caravans, each sleeping six, are also on site. The site also offers a tennis court, games room and safe play area. A lovely farm walk is waymarked

round the site, and there are two golf courses nearby. The site also features a small shop, and several pubs within walking distance. For anyone seeking a rural haven amid great natural beauty and tranquil surroundings, this

**Ashe Farm Caravan and Camping, Ashe, Thornfalcon, Taunton, Somerset TA3 5NW Tel: 01823 442567 Fax: 01823 443372**

is a good site to choose.

## ELM GROVE
2 miles E of Taunton off J25 of the M5

MAP 2 REF E6

**The Old Vicarage** offers self-catering accommodation for visitors. On the edge of Taunton town centre in a quiet residential area, it is within easy reach of the Quantock and Brendon Hills, Exmoor, the coast and all the attractions of Taunton itself and the surrounding area. This 19th-century house, a former vicarage of St James Church, is set to one side of a Victorian square. The accommodation comprises a completely self-contained maisonette with separate entrance within the main house. Furnished in a warm and welcoming style, on the first floor is the kitchen, dining room and spacious,

**The Old Vicarage, Elm Grove, Taunton, Somerset TA1 1EH Tel: 01823 284877 Fax: 01823 353559 e-mail: ovdlh@aol.com**

comfortable lounge. The second floor has the bathroom with shower and two bedrooms - one with twin beds, the other with a double bed. Bed linen, towels, heating and electricity are all included in the charge. No smoking. Pay phone. Sorry, no pets.

# VALE OF TAUNTON DEANE

## CHEDDON FITZPAINE                                    MAP 2 REF E5
2 miles N of Taunton off the A38

In the lanes to the north of Taunton town centre, the beautiful **Hestercombe Gardens** lie on the south-facing foothills of the Quantocks just north of the village of Cheddon Fitzpaine. This carefully-restored Edwardian garden is an outstanding example of the professional collaboration between the architect, Sir Edwin Lutyens, and the landscape designer, Gertrude Jekyll. Originally laid out in 1904, Hestercombe was restored in the 1980s by Somerset County Council using Jekyll's original planting scheme as a guide.

## NORTON FITZWARREN                                    MAP 2 REF D5
2 miles W of Taunton off the B3227

Farmhouse cider has been made in the countryside around Taunton since time immemorial. The damp fertile land in this part of Somerset is ideal for growing cider apples, and a number of producers, large and small, continue to operate in the area. One of the largest has its factory at Norton Fitzwarren, a scattered village on the B3227, a couple of miles west of Taunton. The remains of an early Bronze Age bank and ditch enclosure can also be made out here, artefacts from which can be seen in the county museum at Taunton Castle.

## BISHOPS LYDEARD                                    MAP 2 REF D5
3 miles NW of Taunton on the A358

The sizable village of Bishops Lydeard lies four miles west of Hestercombe Gardens, off the A358 Williton road. This is the southern terminus of the **West Somerset Railway**, a privately-operated steam railway which runs for almost twenty miles to Minehead on the Bristol Channel coast. The longest line of its kind in the country, it was formed when British Rail's 100-year-old branch between Taunton and Minehead was closed in 1971. After a five-year restoration programme, the new company began operating a limited summer service which has steadily grown in popularity. Special attractions include the first class Pullman dining car and the "Flockton Flyer", a steam locomotive which may be recognised for its many appearances on film and television. Services between the line's ten stations run throughout the day between mid-March and end-October.

COMBE FLOREY                                           MAP 2 REF D5
8 miles NW of Taunton off the A358

**Redlands** is located in a quiet rural setting by a lovely stream and adjacent to the
Quantock Hills. Owners Brian and Elizabeth Totman have been here since 1999
and offer all their guests a warm welcome. Formerly two barns and an old cider
house, the properties were converted in the late 1980s to become the main house
and two self-catering cottages. Guests of all ages and walks of life enjoy the peace

and restfulness of this tranquil spot. Walkers and visitors to the Quantocks and Exmoor, as well as those en route to Minehead, find this a perfect base for exploring the preserved West Somerset Railway, Taunton, Dunster Castle, the Somerset Levels and other sights in this

**Redlands, Treble's Holford, Combe Florey, Taunton,
Somerset TA4 3HA Tel: 01823 433159
e-mail: redlandshouse@hotmail.com
www.escapetothecountry.co.uk**

part of Somerset. Both Bed and Breakfast and self-catering accommodation are
available here. The two en-suite guest bedrooms - one bedroom in the main
house plus one bedroom with facilities for people with disabilities downstairs -
are furnished and decorated in the best style and quality.

Breakfast is notable for both its quantity and superb quality, whether guests
choose the traditional English or Continental breakfast. There are also two self-
catering cottages, each with its own entrance and private garden area with tables,
chairs and barbecue. Both cottages are equipped to a high standard with fitted
kitchens and bathrooms and are suitable for round-the-year occupation. Cider
Cottage has a pretty gallery bedroom with exposed roof timbers and sleeps two
people or can be used for a family with a young child. Redlands Barn has a
comfortable beamed open-plan living/dining room with well equipped kitchen.
There are two bedrooms - one double, one twin - and an additional folding bed
and cot can be provided. Guests have use of a utility room with automatic wash-

ing machine, tumble dryer and freezer. Table tennis and gorgeous gardens are also available for guests to enjoy.

## WELLINGTON

MAP 2 REF D6

6 miles SW of Taunton on the B3187

The old market town of Wellington lies beside the A38, six miles southwest of Taunton. **The Green Dragon** in the town centre of Wellington offers good food, drink and accommodation in comfortable and hospitable surroundings. This relaxing and welcoming pub dates back to the 15th century, and was built as a traditional coaching inn. The old stables can still be seen to the rear of the pub. The main bar boasts many original features and a warm and friendly ambience. From the old living quarters on ground level, a stylish and pleasant new restaurant has been created. From sandwiches and bar snacks to main courses using the freshest local ingredients, the menu offers a good range of options. All-day breakfasts, steaks, chicken dishes, curries, fish and filled baguettes are just some of the choices on offer. The well-stocked bar has a variety of beers, wines and spirits. There are also three charming and comfortable guest bedrooms. Owners Ruth and Brian Pike and their helpful, friendly staff make any visit here a pleasant one.

**The Green Dragon, 23 South Street, Wellington, Somerset TA21 8NR Tel: 01823 662281**

Once an important producer of woven cloth and serge, the prosperity of Wellington owed much to Quaker entrepreneurs, and later, the Fox banking family. (Fox, Fowler and Co were the last private bank in England to issue notes, continuing to do so until 1921 when they were taken over by Lloyds.) The broad streets around the centre are peppered with fine Georgian buildings, including the neoclassical town hall, and at the eastern end of the town there is a much-altered Perpendicular-style church which contains the ostentatious tomb of Sir John Popham, the judge who presided at the trial of Guy Fawkes. Another spectacular monument, that to the Duke of Wellington, can be seen on a spur of the

Blackdown Hills, three miles to the south; more is written about this in the chapter on South Somerset. Present-day Wellington is a pleasant and prosperous shopping and light industrial centre which enjoys easy access to and from the M5.

**The Ship Inn** is a lively and welcoming inn on the edge of Wellington, near the Wellington Monument. Built of traditional stone in the 1700s, this venerable coaching inn has a large L-shaped open-plan bar area, with comfortable seating and an attractive decor featuring prints of seafaring scenes. There are always at least two real ales on tap, along with a good complement of beers, wines and spirits. The food available offers good value for money, with a hearty and tasty range of sandwiches and main courses such as chicken dishes, steaks and much more. In summer, cream teas can be taken in the lovely garden area. Accommodation is also on hand, in one of two cosy guest bedrooms, decorated and furnished in keeping with the style throughout the inn. Owner Tammie Lynne Lewis and her staff make all guests feel most welcome. Open: Monday to Friday 12-2.30 and 6 - 11; all day Saturday; Sundays 12-3 and 7-10.30.

**The Ship Inn, 39 Mantle Street, Wellington, Somerset TA21 8AX Tel/Fax: 01823 662106**

## THORNE ST MARGARET
8 miles SW of Taunton off the A38

MAP 1 REF D6

The Vale of Taunton Deane, the broad valley between the southern Quantocks and the Devon border, contains some of the most fertile farmland in the county. Thanks to its prolonged agricultural prosperity, the area is dotted with fine country houses. Three that are worthy of note can be found to the west of Wellington in the lanes around the village of Thorne St Margaret. **Cothay Manor**, described by Pevsner as "one of the most perfect smaller English manor houses of the late 15th century", stands beside the River Tone a mile to the west of the village; the gardens in particular are worth seeing. The slightly older **Greenham Barton**, which retains its early 15th-century two-storey porch and open hall, is situated a mile to the south; and **Wellisford Manor**, which was built of brick around 1700 in a style reflecting the contemporary architecture of nearby Devon, lies half a mile to the north.

## WIVELISCOMBE
MAP 1 REF D5

10 miles NW of Taunton on the B3227

Another large village, Wiveliscombe, lies on the B3227 three miles to the north-west of Milverton. An ancient settlement with a strangely remote atmosphere, the Romans once occupied a fort here and indeed, they left behind a quantity of 3rd and 4th-century coins to prove it. In medieval times, the local manor house was a summer residence of the bishops of Bath and Wells. Its remains, which include a striking 14th-century archway, have now been incorporated into a group of cottages near the church. The red sandstone church was totally rebuilt in the 19th century in a curious neo-Gothic style which is part-Perpendicular, part-18th-century preaching house. During the Second World War, the crypt was used to store priceless historic documents and ecclesiastical treasures which were brought here from parts of the country which were more at risk from aerial attack.

Specialising in cask-conditioned beers from regional and local brewers, **The Bear Inn** is a lively and welcoming public house that began life as a coaching inn in the 1600s. Refurbished and renovated several times over the years, it maintains a comfortable and traditional feel. The large L-shaped open-plan bar has beamed ceilings and Tudor-style wall timbers. Brasses, copper implements and an interesting collection of table mats adorn the walls and ceiling beams. There are five

**The Bear Inn, 10 North Street, Wiveliscombe, Somerset TA4 2JY
Tel: 01984 623537**

handsome guest bedrooms (four twins and one double), which reflect in their size and structure the architecture of the 17th century, with sloping ceilings and floors adding to the homely olde worlde ambience of this characterful establishment. There are always at least seven real ales on tap, including two from a local brewery. The meals are home-cooked using fresh local produce, and are served either in the bar or in the separate restaurant area. The menu boasts a variety of traditional favourites, from snacks to tempting meals such as steak and kidney pie or mixed grill, together with vegetarian and fish dishes.

**Greenway Farm** is a working goat farm set in 125 acres in an area of outstanding beauty. Situated high on a natural hill on the edge of Wiveliscombe, it is surrounded by rolling hills. Providing milk for cheesemaking, this lovely countryside setting is home to a 150-year-old stonebuilt farmhouse offering bed and breakfast accommodation. Furnished in period style, throughout, there are three lovely and comfortable guest bedrooms as well as an attractive and welcoming guests' lounge. The rooms are high-ceilinged, spacious and charming. A true home from home atmosphere pervades this superior establishment. Guests can enjoy a relaxing and peaceful stay, or if they choose take part in a number of country pursuits available,

**Greenway Farm, Wiveliscombe, Taunton,
Somerset TA4 2UA
Tel: 01984 623359 Fax: 01984 624051**

including walking, game, coarse or sea fishing, and riding. The home-cooked breakfast is delicious; evening meals are also available by arrangement. This pristine and traditional farmhouse makes a welcome retreat for any short or long holiday. Owner Mary Woollaston is a welcoming and conscientious host. ETB 3 Diamonds

## TOLLAND
10 miles NW of Taunton off the B3224

Map 1 ref D5

The B3188 to the north of Wiveliscombe passes to the west of Tolland, the location of the lovely **Gaulden Manor**. The estate dates from the 12th century, although the present house is largely 17th century. It once belonged to the Turberville family, a name borrowed by Thomas Hardy for use in his novel, *Tess of the D'Urbervilles*.

**Gaulden Manor, Tolland**

Still in use as a family home, the house contains an exceptional collection of period furniture and fine china. The great hall has a superb plaster ceiling and fireplace, and the room known as the chapel boasts a particularly fine oak screen.

Set in a beautiful wooded combe, Gaulden Manor is surrounded by a series of small ornamental enclosures known as the "Little Gardens of Gaulden". These include a scent garden, butterfly garden, rose garden, bog garden and Old Monk's fish pond.

## MILVERTON
6 miles W of Taunton on the B3187

Map 1 ref D5

The B3187 to the north of Wellington leads to the sizable village of Milverton, another former weaving centre which has been left with a legacy of elegant Georgian houses. The largely 14th-century red sandstone **Church of St Michael** contains some striking internal features, including a Norman font with characteristic cross and cable carving, a set of choir stalls carved with the twelve apostles, a handsome rood screen, and some fine carved bench ends.

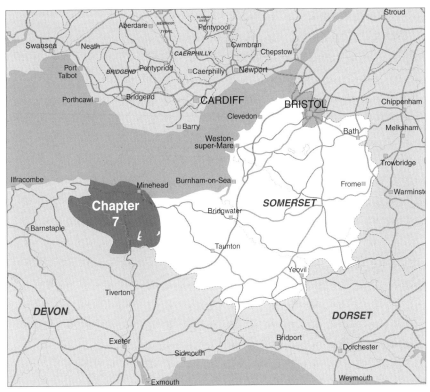

© MAPS IN MINUTES ™ (1998)

## BRENDON HILLS TO THE COAST

### MONKSILVER
6 miles SE of Minehead off the A358

MAP 1 REF C5

Another handsome manor house lies the southern edge of Monksilver, three miles to the north on the B3188 Watchet road. Built in the middle of Elizabeth I's reign on the site of a monastic settlement, **Combe Sydenham Hall** was the home of Elizabeth Sydenham, first wife of Sir Francis Drake. According to local legend, after Elizabeth had consented to the marriage, she grew so weary of waiting for Sir Francis to return from his voyages around the world that she resolved to wed another. While on her way to the church, however, a meteorite flew out of the sky and smashed into the ground in front of her, a sign, she thought, that she ought to wait on. The original meteorite, now known as "Drake's Cannonball", is on display in the great hall and is said to bring luck to those who touch it. The 500-acre grounds have been designated a country park and contain a working corn mill complete with water wheel, an Elizabethan-style garden, woodland walks, children's play area and deer park.

The estate also incorporates a modern trout farm which stands on the site of a fully restored Tudor trout hatchery dating from the end of the 16th century. Here, visitors can purchase fresh rainbow trout, smoked trout and a number of other specialist food products made here under the "Monksmill" label. **Nettlecombe Court**, one mile to the west, is an ancient manor which once belonged to the Raleigh family, relations of Sir Walter. Later, it passed by marriage to the Cornish Trevelyans, and it is now a field studies centre which is open to visitors on Thursdays only by appointment.

## TREBOROUGH                                                    MAP 1 REF C5
6 miles S of Minehead off A39

Towards Treborough, the land rises into the **Brendon Hills**, the upland area within the Exmoor National Park lying to the east and north of the River Exe. During the mid 19th century, iron ore was mined in significant quantities above the village of Treborough, then carried down a steep mineral railway to the coast for shipment to the furnaces of South Wales. At one time almost 1000 people were employed by the Ebbw Vale Company, strict Nonconformists who imposed a rigorous teetotal regime on their workers. (Those wanting a drink had to walk across the moor all the way to Raleigh's Cross.)

The company also founded a miners' settlement with a temperance hotel and three chapels, which became renowned for the achievements of its choir and fife and drum band. Sections of the old mineral railway can still be made out today, such as the one near the junction of the A39 and the B3190 to the east of Washford, and the two-mile stretch leading down to the coast at Watchet is now a pleasant footpath. The Brendon Hills also offer some fine walking through attractive woodland and open moorland, and further south, the surprisingly well-assimilated **Wimbleball and Clatworthy Reservoirs** offer some good facilities for picnickers, anglers and watersports enthusiasts.

## STOGUMBER                                                    MAP 1 REF D5
6 miles SE of Minehead off the A358

The lanes to the east of Monksilver lead through the curiously-named village of Stogumber to Stogumber Halt, one of ten stations on the West Somerset Railway.

**Bee World and Animal Centre** near Stogumber Station on the West Somerset Railway is a unique hands-on rare breeds and nature centre. Visitors are

welcome to join in at feeding times, pet the animals (or even cuddle some of the smaller ones, like the rabbits and guinea pigs), and take part in turning out the animals, ferret racing and other fun and educational activities. Family-run by Richard Bolton, a life-long bee-

**Bee World and Animal Centre, Stogumber Station, Lower Water, Somerset TA4 3TR Tel: 01984 656545 website: www.scoot.co.uk/bee_world**

keeper, and his wife and son, the centre has expanded organically and continues to grow. Visitor attractions are added year on year, such as (new for 1999) an undercover games area and crazy golf course; guided tours and illustrated talks are also available. This extensive centre offers acres of sights, sounds and activities, making for a wonderful day out for all the family. At the bee demonstrations, visitors can watch working hives in complete safety (the bees are kept behind glass at all times). There's also a picnic area, woodland walks and "the honey trail", which follows the process from pollen collection to extracting honey from the hive. Near the Wild Lake, sightings have been reported of kingfishers, herons, mallards, little grebes, tufted ducks, sedgewarblers, moorhens and nine species of dragon flies and damsel flies. In the farm shop, natural honey- and bee-based products including candles, face and hand creams, potted honey and other mementos, including post cards, are sold. The Tea Rooms/restaurant serves delicious home-made snacks and light lunches, such as soups, honey-cured ham and vegetarian dishes, as well as tea, coffee, and soft drinks. Craft demonstrations, the video room and the safe play and adventure playground areas complete the marvellous amenities at this comprehensive farming centre. Open: Easter until the end of October, seven days a week, 10 - dusk. Open all year round for groups, by appointment.

## CROWCOMBE
MAP 1 REF D4

8 miles SE of Minehead off the A358

One of the loveliest villages in the area, Crowcombe, is situated in the western foothills of the Quantocks, to the east of Stogumber station and the A358 Taunton to Williton road. Once an important stopping place on the road to the Bristol

Channel coast, the village has an impressive mainly Perpendicular parish church with a fan-vaulted south porch, a fine south aisle, and a wonderful collection of bench ends, one of which is dated 1534, depicting such curious pagan-looking figures as the green man, a mermaid, and a pair of naked men attempting to spear a dragon. A striking 17th-century family pew of the Carews can be seen in the north transept, and there is also an 18th-century screen, pulpit and altar designed by Thomas Parker.

Parker was also the architect of **Crowcombe Court**, the somewhat down-at-heel looking brick mansion which dominates the village. However, he wasn't able to see his commission through to completion for he was dismissed in 1734 because of rocketing building costs (£4,122). The village also contains a rare part-Tudor church house which served as a parish hall, and a Jacobean brewery with mullioned windows whose lower floor was later converted to almshouses and whose upper floor became a school.

WILLITON                                                    MAP 1 REF D4
6 miles SE of Minehead on the A39

To the northwest of Crowcombe, the A358 runs along the foot of the Quantock ridge to its junction with the A39 at Williton, a former Saxon royal estate which is now a sizable village on the busy holiday route to Minehead and the west Somerset coast. The manor was the home of Sir Reginald FitzUrse, one of Thomas Becket's murderers, who donated half the manor to the Knights Templar to expiate his leading role. The other half of the main manor continued in the FitzUrse family until the death of Sir Ralph FitzUrse in 1350, when it was divided between his daughters.

After 14 years as a potter, Martin Pettinger set up **Williton Pottery** in Half Acre in 1982,

**Williton Pottery, Half Acre, Williton, Somerset TA4 4NZ Tel: 01984 632150**

specialising in a style called slip ware. Slips (liquid colour clays) have been used to decorate pots in England since the 16th century. This process involves sieving coloured clays to the consistency of emulsion paint, then pouring them over a slightly damp raw red clay pot. The results are astonishingly beautiful. The gallery area showcases a select display of exhibition-standard pots, while the main showroom offers a wealth of carefully made pots, all individual and diverse. All items are for sale, and pots may be commissioned. Martin is a Craft member of the Somerset Guild of Craftsmen and the West Country Potters Association. Buyers can therefore be assured of the finest quality.

Present-day Williton contains the diesel locomotive workshops of the **West Somerset Railway**, and just off the A39 at **Orchard Mill**, there is a restored water wheel and **The Bakelite Museum** - a must for any fan of this truly amazing man-made wonder, the "pioneer of plastics". A delightful small country manor house, Orchard Wyndham, is situated a mile to the southwest of the village. Built in the 14th century and much-altered since, it has been used as a family home by the Wyndhams for the past four and a half centuries.

**The Egremont Hotel** in the centre of town is a distinguished old coaching inn that was originally called The Blue Anchor - a name that indicates that it was once a smugglers' haunt. In 1720 it became known as The Coach and Horses, and featured stabling for up to 36 horses. Additions to the building were constructed in the 19th century, and it was given its present name in 1843, to honour the last Earl of Egremont, still living at that time. The present owners, Andrew and Angela Yon, have given it a fresh coat of paint and made many improvements and changes, while retaining the hotel's traditional feel and welcoming ambience. Offering great food, drink, accommodation and hospitality, there are two

**The Egremont Hotel, 1 Fore Street, Williton, Somerset TA4 4PX  Tel: 01984 632500  Fax: 01984 633377**

comfortable bars and a restaurant area. Open fires and excellent furnishings and decor enhance the hotel's comfort and relaxation. Everything from morning coffee through snacks and a fine a la carte menu offer guests a wealth of choice.

The menu features Indian and Indonesian specialities as well as more traditional favourites. This characterful hotel has 10 guest bedrooms, each furnished and decorated to a high standard of taste and comfort.

## SAMPFORD BRETT                                      MAP 1 REF D4
6 miles SE of Minehead off the A358

Sampford Brett has a long and proud history. Recorded in the Domesday Book, its name derives from both the sandy ford which crossed the Doniford stream between this village and Woolaston, and from the heirs of Sir Simon de Bret; his descendant, Sir Adam de Brett first obtained a charter for a weekly market (in 1306). Today it remains a lovely and unspoilt village. The handsome parish church of St George dates back to the 13th century, with later additions.

**Elmfield** is a large detached village house dating back to the early 18th century - registered in 1703 as "No. 1 Gentleman's Residence". This characterful house is built of local stone. Here owner Margaret Fountain, a conscientious and welcoming host, offers superb bed and breakfast accommodation. There are three charming and comfortable guest bedrooms, one of which is en suite. Sunny and south-facing, clean and spacious, they offer guests every modern amenity in tranquil and relaxing surroundings.

**Elmfield, Sampford Brett, Somerset  TA4 4JY**
**Tel: 01984 632315  Fax: 01984 632550**
**e-mail: m.fountain@elmfieldsb.freeserve.co.uk**

The residents' lounge is also lovely, with beautiful furnishings in period style. Nestling below the spectacular Quantock Hills, guests here can enjoy a real taste of peaceful village life. The flower-filled courtyard is just the place to take breakfast or enjoy a rest at any time on fine days, and leads to one acre of formal and informal gardens. Indoors there are welcoming log fires that enhance the cosy, homely atmosphere.

## WASHFORD

Map 1 ref C4

4 miles SE of Minehead on the A39

At Washford, two miles west of Williton, a lane to the south of the A39 leads to the remains of **Cleeve Abbey**, the only monastery in Somerset to have belonged to the austere Cistercian order. The abbey was founded in 1198 by the Earl of Lincoln in the beautiful valley of the River Washford, or *Vallis Florida*. Many of the great monastic houses were allowed to fall into disrepair following Henry VIII's Dissolution of the Monasteries in 1539. However, the cloister buildings at Cleeve were soon put to domestic use and are now among the most complete in the country.

Despite the cruciform abbey church having been reduced to its foundations, the refectory, chapter house, monks' common room, dormitory and cloisters remain remarkably intact. Most impressive of all is the great hall, a magnificent building with tall windows and a wagon roof which is decorated with busts of crowned angels, moulded wall plates, medieval murals, and a unique set of floor tiles with heraldic designs. The curved dormitory staircase with its archways and mullioned windows is particularly fine, and the combined gatehouse and almonry, the last building to be constructed before the Dissolution, makes an imposing entrance to the abbey precinct.

Somewhat less venerable, but still enjoyable, attractions in Washford include **Tropiquaria** - as its name suggests, this wildlife park features tropical animals; there's also an aquarium, aviary and the chance for visitors to stroke snakes, handle tarantulas and in many other ways get in touch with their wilder side - and the **Torre Cider Farm** - admission free.

## WATCHET

Map 1 ref D4

4 miles E of Minehead on the Coast

Watchet, a small town on the coast to the north of Washford, has been a port since Saxon times. In the 6th century, St Decuman is reputed to have landed here from Wales, bringing with him a cow to provide sustenance, and in the 10th century, the settlement was important enough to have been sacked by the Vikings on at least three occasions. By the 17th century, Watchet had become an important paper manufacturing centre, and by the mid 19th, around 30,000 tons of iron ore from the Brendon hills were being exported each year through its docks. Coleridge's imaginary crew set sail from here in "**The Rime Of The Ancient Mariner**", the epic poem which was written when the author was residing at nearby Nether Stowey.

Unlike many similar-sized ports which fell into disuse following the arrival of the railways, **Watchet docks** has somehow managed to survive. Despite the total decline in the iron ore trade, sizable cargo vessels continue to tie up here to be loaded with goods bound for the Iberian peninsula and elsewhere.

The scale of Watchet's parish church reflects the town's long-standing importance. Set well away from the centre, it contains several fine tombs to members of the Wyndham family, the local lords of the manor who did much to develop the economic potential of the locality. Rumour has it that one 16th-century family member, Florence Wyndham, had to be buried twice: the day after her first funeral, the church sexton went down to the vaults to surreptitiously remove a ring from her finger and the old woman suddenly woke up. In recent years, Watchet has also developed as something of a coastal resort whose attractions include an interesting small museum dedicated to local maritime history.

**The Bell Inn** is a distinguished and welcoming public house with an impressive history. An important landmark in the tradition of English literature, it is recorded that the first lines of Samuel Taylor Coleridge's *Rhyme of the Ancient Mariner* were put to paper at the inn, while he was staying, along with William Wordsworth, at the inn in the winter of 1797. For over 200 years the inn has been the meeting place of the Court Leet of the 'town and borough' of Watchet, a survivor of the days when the local government of a town or district was conducted by the townspeople themselves. Refurbished in recent years, this handsome pub retains its tradi-

The Bell Inn, 3 Market Street, Watchet, Somerset
TA23 0AN  Tel: 01984 631279

tional feel and cosy ambience. There's good range of refreshment on offer, from lagers, wines and spirits to delicious meals and snacks, home-cooked and prepared to order. Owners Ken and Norma Wilkinson and their staff provide friendly hospitality and excellent service to all their guests.

## BLUE ANCHOR BAY
3 miles E of Minehead on the Coast

MAP 1 REF C4

Another seaside resort can be found three miles to the west at Blue Anchor Bay, a broad arc of sand named after a 17th-century inn, not the colour of the water. One of the resort's attractions is **Home Farm**, on the seafront, which offers hands-on experience of farming life, with friendly farm animals, woodland walks, wildflower meadows and more.

## CARHAMPTON
3 miles SE of Minehead on the A39

MAP 1 REF C4

The atmosphere is very different at Carhampton, one mile to the southwest, a small inland village on the A39 which was the site of a Viking victory in the 9th century. The original church was named after St Carantoc, an early Celtic missionary from across the Bristol Channel who is reputed to have chosen the site for his ministry by throwing his stone altar overboard and following it to the shore. The present structure, though much restored, contains a remarkable 15th-century painted screen which extends across the entire church. The old inn near the churchyard lych gate has the date 1638 set into its cobbled floor in sheep's knuckle bones.

Each January, the residents of Carhampton re-enact the ancient custom of "**wassailing the apple trees**". A toast is made to the most productive tree in the district and cider is poured onto its trunk in a charming ceremony which is probably pagan in origin. A local folk tale tells of mysterious Madame Carne, a Carhampton woman who died in 1612 after having done away with three husbands. According to the legend, her ghost returned home after her funeral to prepare breakfast for the mourners.

A very warm and friendly welcome awaits visitors to **The Butcher's Arms** in Carhampton, a charming public house dating back to the 1500s. This traditional coaching inn combines the historic and modern. The only pub selling 'Wassail' in the country, it is a popular and locally renowned place famous for its hospitality, fine ales and great food. The beer garden is equipped with a barbecue for summer feasts and a safe and attractive children's play area. The interior is comfortable and handsome, as befits the former home of 16th-century monks. Attractive features include the floor of the bar, made of 'Sheep's Knuckles' and dating to 1658, and the fireplace base, made from old ships' timbers. The bar snacks and menu offer a variety of delicious and freshly prepared meals and refreshments, and the Sunday roast is justly popular. There are always three real ales on tap, as well as an excellent range of lagers, wines and spirits.

**The Butcher's Arms, Main Road, Carhampton,
nr Minehead, Somerset TA24 6LP Tel: 01643 821333**

## BILBROOK
MAP 1 REF C4

5 miles SE of Minehead off the A39

**The Dragon House** in Bilbrook is a distinguished and comfortable hotel and restaurant run by three generations of the Napper family. Dating from the 17th century, the house is set in three acres of beautiful grounds on the edge of Exmoor. This historic country house hotel boasts 10 handsome en suite guest bedrooms, including doubles, twins and family rooms. Whilst keeping their individual charm, the rooms have all been discreetly modernised to offer all the modern traveller's requirements. The spacious guests' lounge is furnished in period style. The grounds include an impressive Black Poplar, the oldest and largest in England. Within easy distance of Dunster, Minehead and Exmoor, this delightful establishment makes a perfect base for sightseeing. The oak-panelled restaurant is the perfect setting to enjoy

**The Dragon House, Bilbrook, nr Minehead, Somerset TA24 6HQ Tel: 01984 640215 Fax: 01984 641340 e-mail: info@dragonhouse.co.uk**

the varied and professional menu, with dishes based on classic Continental and West Country cuisine. Fresh local produce is used wherever possible, and the wine list is superb. Light meals, bar snacks, drinks and other refreshments are served in the bar, conservatory, or attractive colonnaded courtyard.

## TIMBERSCOMBE
MAP 1 REF C4

3 miles S of Minehead off the A396

Set in the centre of the lovely village of Timberscombe, **The Lion Inn** is a traditional public house dating back to the 15th century when it was a coaching inn. Owners Lillian, Simon and Andy are friendly and welcoming hosts. They have recently purchased the pub, but bring a wealth of experience in catering. This friendly and comfortable family-run pub boasts open fires in the main bar, res-

The Lion Inn, Church Street, Timberscombe, Dunster, Somerset TA24 7TP  Tel: 01643 841243

taurant and lounge/restaurant. The open-plan main bar has an oak L-shaped bar and half-panelled walls and is adorned with brasses and other memorabilia. The Exmoor Lounge Restaurant has a varied lunch and evening menu of traditional and more innovative favourites such as home-made soup - served with the bread Lillian herself bakes fresh every day - steaks, chilli con carne, chicken, lamb, salmon and pasta dishes and mushroom stroganoff. There are also tempting daily specials. The bar offers a good range of lagers, wines and spirits.

## DUNSTER  MAP 1 REF C4
2 miles S of Minehead on the A396

The ancient fortified settlement of Dunster has an almost fairy-tale appearance when approached along the A39 from the southeast. With its huge turreted castle rising above the trees and distinctive ruined folly on nearby Conygar hill, it is a place well-worth visiting, particularly out of season. **Dunster Castle** was founded by William de Mohun on a natural promontory above the River Avill a few years before the Domesday Book was compiled in 1086. In 1404, it passed to the Luttrells for the then colossal sum of 5000 marks, about £3300, in whose family it remained until Lt. Col. G W F Luttrell presented the property to the National Trust in 1975.

During the English Civil War, Dunster Castle was one of the last Royalist strongholds in the West Country to fall, the garrison finally surrendering after a siege lasting 160 days. The castle underwent some major alterations during the latter part of the 17th century and some of its finest internal features date from this period, including the superb plasterwork ceiling in the dining room, and the magnificent balustraded main staircase with its delicately-carved flora and fauna. The banqueting hall contains a unique collection of 16th-century leather hangings, and there are also many fine examples of period furniture throughout the interior.

Further changes to the building by Anthony Salvin in the 19th century completed the transformation from castle to country mansion. Work on the steeply-terraced garden with its striking collection of rare shrubs and subtropical plants was also carried out at this time. Dunster Castle is surrounded by an attractive 28-acre park containing an 18th-century flour mill which was built on the site of a Norman predecessor. Restored to working order in 1979, **Dunster Working Water Mill** continues to produce flour and other cereals for wholesale and retail sale.

The old feudal settlement of Dunster has a wide main street which is dominated by the castle. At the northern end stands the former **Yarn Market**, a small octagonal building erected by the Luttrells around 1600 when the village was a centre of the cloth trade. Indeed, such was its importance that at one time, Dunster gave its name to a type of woollen cloth which was renowned for its quality and strength. The nearby **Luttrell Arms** is over a century older; a private residence which was converted to an inn around 1650, it has a fine 15th-century porch and a room lined with carved oak panelling. It once belonged to Cleeve Abbey, as did the 14th-century nunnery in Church Street. Dunster's principal medieval monastic house, **Dunster Priory**, was an outpost of Bath Abbey. Now largely demolished, the only parts to survive are its splendid priory church and unusual 12th-century dovecote. This can be seen in a nearby garden and still contains the revolving ladder which was used to reach the roosting birds.

Dunster's former priory church is now one of the finest parish churches in

**Dunster Yarn Market**

Somerset. Rebuilt of rose pink sandstone by the monks after 1100, its 100ft tower was added in the 15th century at a cost of 13s 4d per foot, with an extra 20s for the pinnacles. The building's most outstanding internal feature is its fan vaulted rood screen which extends across the nave and aisles, one of the widest and most impressive of its kind in the country. There are also some fine 15th and 16th-century fittings, an unusual painting of the Brazen Serpent thought to be by Thornhill, and several monuments to members of the Luttrell family. On the southern edge of the village, the River Avill is spanned by the ancient **Gallox Bridge**, a medieval packhorse bridge which is now under the care of English Heritage.

Dunster's Memorial Hall is home to the lovely **Dolls Museum**, with over 700 dolls from different periods and countries, dressed in delightful outfits and national costumes.

# MINEHEAD

Two miles to the northwest of Dunster, the West Somerset Railway terminates at Minehead, a popular seaside town lying at the foot of the wooded promontory known as **North Hill**. Despite sounding like a product of the industrial age, this is one of the oldest settlements in the county, having been a busy Bristol Channel port since the time of the Celts. The old harbour lies in the lee of North Hill, making it one of the safest landing places in the West Country. At one time, ships would arrive here with their cargoes of wool and livestock from Ireland, crops from the plantations of Virginia, coal from the valleys of South Wales, and day trippers from Cardiff and Bristol. Today, however, the merchantmen and paddle steamers have gone and the harbour is the peaceful haunt of sailing dinghies and pleasure craft.

A good view of the old port can be had from the **North Hill Nature Trail**, a three-mile walk which starts near the lifeboat station on the harbourside. Minehead's parish church of St Michael stands in a prominent position below North Hill. A substantial part 14th-century building, in past centuries a light was kept burning in the tower to help guide ships into the harbour. The interior contains a number of unusual features, including a rare medieval prayer book, or missal, which once belonged to the Richard Fitzjames, a local vicar who went on to become Bishop of London in 1506.

Minehead's 19th-century decline as a port was offset by its gradual expansion as a seaside resort. The local powers that be went to great pains to attract a suitably respectable clientele, and indeed a local bylaw was in force until 1890 which forbad anyone over ten years of age from swimming in the sea "except from a bathing machine, tent, or other effective screen." The arrival of the railway in 1874 failed to trigger the brutal expansion experienced by some other seaside resorts, and during the First World War, Minehead was able to provide an escape from the ravages of war at timeless establishments like the Strand Hotel, where guests were entertained by such stars as Anna Pavlova and Gladys Cooper.

High on a hill to the northwest of Minehead town centre, overlooking the bay, **"Beverleigh"** is a comfortable guest house with three lovely guest bedrooms offering superb views over the surrounding countryside, from Exmoor to the Quantocks. The bedrooms are large and tastefully furnished; one room has a luxurious four-poster bed. This charming Edwardian home sits within one-third of an acre of mature gardens with winding pathways, mature trees and secluded lawns. Furnished in period style throughout, there's a spacious and welcoming guests' lounge. A warm and friendly homely atmosphere pervades this charming establishment. Decorative wall hangings, handsome photographs and owner Jannie Bakker's own mementos and knick knacks enhance

**"Beverleigh"**, Beacon Road, Minehead, Somerset TA24 5SF Tel: 01643 708450

the informal and comfortable ambience. The traditional cooked breakfast (or vegetarian option) is excellent and hearty, setting guests up well for a day's sight-seeing or exploring Minehead and the countryside or coast. Open all year round.

Improvements to Minehead have been gradual. The most momentous change came in 1962 when Billy Butlin opened a holiday camp at the eastern end of the esplanade. Now updated and renamed **Somerwest World**, this popular attraction has done much to transform present-day Minehead into an all-round family resort.

Set high on the hill behind the town centre, two minutes from the centre and overlooking the bay, within minutes of magnificent walks to Selworthy and adjacent to the lovely St Michael's Church, **Marston Lodge Hotel** is a distinguished and welcoming Edwardian building purpose built as an hotel. There are 10 beautifully furnished en suite guest bedrooms (non-smoking), all spacious

and supremely comfortable. The hotel also boasts a handsome residents' lounge and lovely dining room. The menu offers an impressive variety of starters and main courses, all freshly prepared and using fresh produce from the garden. There's an extensive wine list and a tempting selection of desserts, well worth leaving

**Marston Lodge Hotel, St Michael's Road, North Hill, Minehead, Somerset TA24 5JP Tel/Fax: 01643 702510**

room for! The acre of landscaped gardens are a haven of peace and natural beauty, with shrubs, flower beds and borders, summerhouse and enclosed patio. Guests are also welcome to concessions on offer at the nearby golf course.

## MINEHEAD TO THE EXMOOR NATIONAL PARK

SELWORTHY                                                          Map 1 ref B4
3 miles W of Minehead off the A39

For those wishing to avoid Minehead's summer crush, a particularly fine walk sets out westwards over North Hill and continues on to **Selworthy Beacon**, part of the 12,400-acre Holnicote Estate. The estate covers four and a half miles of coastline between Minehead and Porlock Bay and is now owned by the National Trust. At Hurlstone Point, the South West Coast Path curves inland to avoid the possibility of landslips in the soft Foreland Sandstone before dropping down to Bossington; however, there is an alternative, more arduous clifftop path which should be attempted by experienced walkers only.

The Holnicote Estate extends over five miles inland to the 1,700-foot Dunkery Beacon, the highest point on Exmoor. It also incorporates fifteen farms, many of them on the high moor, and a number of small settlements, including Selworthy, a superb model village of whitewashed cob and thatch cottages which was built by Sir Thomas Dyke-Acland to house his estate workers. The churchyard on the hill offers a fine view of Dunkery Beacon, and there is also a National Trust information centre here which is open daily, 10am (2pm Sundays) to 5pm between late-March and end-October.

ALLERFORD                                                               MAP 1 REF B4
5 miles W of Minehead on the A39

Allerford, one mile to the west, is a lovely old village which has some fine stone cottages and an elegant twin-arched **Packhorse Bridge.** Located in Allerford's old school, the **Allerford Museum (The West Somerset Rural Life Museum)** is an imaginatively presented trove of rural life whose exhibits include a Victorian kitchen, laundry and dairy, and an old schoolroom complete with desks, books and children's toys. From Allerford, it is possible to climb back up the hill for the return walk to Minehead, a round trip of about twelve miles. Alternatively, both

**Allerford Packhorse Bridge**

villages can be reached by car from the A39. For those preferring a walk on the high moor, a spectacular circular nature walk starts and finishes at the Webber's Post car park at the foot of Dunkery Hill.

## PORLOCK
MAP 1 REF B4
6 miles W of Minehead off the A39

To the west of Allerford, the A39 winds through the narrow streets of Porlock, an ancient settlement once frequented by Saxon kings which in recent decades has become a popular riding and holiday centre. The village is filled with lovely old buildings, most notably the 15th-century **Dovery Manor** with its striking traceried hall window, and the largely 13th-century red sandstone parish church with its curious truncated shingle spire, the top section of which was lost in a 17th-century thunderstorm. The church also contains an exceptional font, an unusual Easter sepulchre, and a remarkable double tomb consisting of almost life-size alabaster effigies of Sir John Harrington, who was knighted by Henry V during the Agincourt campaign, and his wife, who lived on for over half a century after Sir John's death in 1418.

Porlock has long had the feel of a community at the end of the world thanks to its position at the foot of **Porlock Hill**, the notorious incline which carries the A39 onto Exmoor. The road rises 1,350 feet in under three miles and in places has a gradient of 1 in 4.

## PORLOCK WEIR
MAP 1 REF B4
8 miles W of Minehead off the A39

A less challenging toll road winds its way through the Lovelace estate from **Porlock Weir**, a hamlet lying on the coast a mile and a half to the northwest of Porlock. Now a small tide-affected harbour populated by pleasure craft, this was once an important seaport. The Danes sacked it on a number of occasions in the 10th century, and in 1052, Harold, the future king of England, landed here from Ireland to begin a career which ended at the Battle of Hastings. Now peaceful and picturesque, Porlock Weir offers a number of interesting attractions, including a working blacksmith's forge, a picture gallery, and a glass studio which provides visitors with the opportunity to see lead crystal being made in the traditional manner. A **submerged forest**, a relic of the last Ice Age, lies a short distance offshore and can be glimpsed at low tide.

At Porlock Weir, at the base of Exmoor's rolling hills and within touching distance of the sea front, **Andrews on the Weir** is a gracious and welcoming traditional country-house style restaurant with rooms. Owner Andrew Dixon is a renowned chef who trained in Jersey and has gained experience in some of the best kitchens in the UK. He and his partner Sarah have brought great flair and imagination to this elegant and stylish establishment. They take pride in ensuring that every guest has an enjoyable and relaxing experience here at their labour of love, one of the town's most distinguished restaurants. Popular with visitors to this charming coastal spot, anyone seeking peace and tranquillity amid very comfortable surroundings should head for this welcoming retreat. There are five lovely en suite guest bedrooms, which are spacious and handsome, with excellent furnishings and decor. One has four-poster beds and offers stunning views over the sea. In the well-appointed restaurant, linen sets the tone for a memorable dining experience. The menu offers a delicious and innovative range of starters, main courses and desserts. Dishes such as loin of venison, fillet of Devon

**Andrews on the Weir, Porlock Weir, Porlock, Somerset TA24 8PB Tel: 01643 863300 Fax: 01643 863311**

beef and risotto of artichoke are just a sampling of the tempting choices available at this elegant and attractive restaurant. All dishes are freshly prepared using local ingredients whenever possible. Home-cooked and expertly prepared and presented, they offer a high standard of quality. The service is impeccable. Lunch and dinner are served Tuesday - Saturday; the tempting Sunday lunch is served from midday - 2.30 p.m. For fine dining and superior accommodation, look no further.

## CULBONE
MAP 1 REF B4

8 miles W of Minehead on the A39

From Porlock Weir, a pleasant mile-long walk leads up through the woods to **Culbone Church**, the smallest church in England still in regular use. A true hidden gem which measures only 33ft by 14ft, this superb part-Norman building is set in a delightful wooded combe which once supported a small charcoal-burning community. Inside, there is a fine 14th-century screen and some handsome carved benches.

From Culbone church, the coastal footpath continues on to the Devon border at **County Gate**, one of several spectacular viewpoints on this dramatic stretch of coastline. Here, the great whale's back hills of Exmoor plunge into the sea, giving breathtaking views across the Bristol Channel to South Wales. One of the few Roman remains on Exmoor, a lookout station for observing cross-Channel raiding parties, lies on a headland to the north of the car park.

## DOONE VALLEY
Map 1 ref B4
10 miles W of Minehead off the A39

To the south of County Gate lies the scenic **Doone Valley**, a long enclosed sweep of green pasture and mature woodland which was immortalised by R D Blackmore in his classic romantic novel, Lorna Doone. The now-demolished medieval farm known as Hoccombe Combe is thought to have been the home of a wild and unruly Exmoor family whose real-life exploits provided the inspiration for the story. The beautiful little 15th-century church at Oare is thought to be the setting of the heroine's dramatic interrupted wedding. Inside, there is a fine set of 19th-century box pews and an unusual piscina shaped like a man's head.

## EXMOOR NATIONAL PARK
Map 1 ref B4
SW of Minehead

The characteristic heartland of the Exmoor National Park, seventy per cent of which lies within Somerset, is a high treeless plateau of hard-wearing Devonian shale which has been carved into a series of steep-sided valleys by the prolonged action of the moor's many fast-flowing streams. Whereas the upland vegetation is mostly heather, gorse and bracken, the more sheltered valleys are carpeted with grassy meadows and pockets of woodland. The deep wooded combes also provide shelter for herds of shy red deer which roam at will, but are seldom seen. Easier to spot are the hardy Exmoor ponies, now almost all cross-breeds, which often congregate at roadside parking areas where there can be rich pickings from holidaymakers.

Exmoor is criss-crossed by a network of paths and bridleways which provide some superb opportunities for walking and pony-trekking. Many follow the routes of the ancient ridgeways across the high moor and pass close to the numerous hut circles, standing stones, barrows and other Bronze and Iron Age remains which litter the landscape. Among the finest examples are the stone circle on Porlock Hill, **Alderman's Barrow** north of Exford, and the delightfully-named **Cow Castle** near Simonsbath. The remarkable medieval packhorse bridge known as **Tarr Steps** lies to the north of the village of Hawkridge, near Dulverton. A superb example of a West Country clapper bridge, it is composed of massive flat stones placed across solidly-built dry stone uprights. The Roman relic known as the **Caractacus Stone** can be seen a couple of miles to the east of here near Spire Cross.

## EXFORD
Map 1 ref B5
8 miles SW of Minehead off the B3223/B3224

**Exmoor House Hotel and Restaurant** in Exford is a licensed small family-run hotel overlooking the triangular village green. Here in the geographical centre of Exmoor National Park, on the River Exe, Exford lives up to its claim to be 'capital

**Exmoor House Hotel and Restaurant, Chapel Street, Exford, Minehead, Somerset TA24 7PY Tel: 01643 831304**

of Exmoor'. The village church sits high on a hill. The river runs 20 feet wide and is crossed by a fine triple-arched bridge. Wild trout and salmon run in season. Some 200 years old and built of local stone, this fine hotel boasts four charming and very comfortable en suite bedrooms. The restaurant and tea garden are adjacent to the hotel in the former chapel (dating back to 1833). The restaurant is resplendent with murals depicting local Exmoor scenes, created by local artist Shan Miller. Owner Graham Phillips and his wife offer a high standard of service, and are very welcoming and conscientious hosts. The imaginative menu offers home-cooked and home-prepared traditional favourites from light snacks and sandwiches to plaice stuffed with broccoli and cheese, steak and kidney pie, and home-made lasagne. A full drinks service is available from the licensed bar when any main meal is ordered. The Sunday roasts and summer barbecues are perennially popular. Prior booking is essential. The cream teas are also justly renowned, with tempting home-made scones, fruit cake, shortbread and tea cakes, lashings of jam and prize-winning clotted cream. The tea is blended locally by Miles of Porlock; coffee, hot chocolate, milkshakes and other cold drinks are also served. Exford is an excellent base from which to explore the delights of the Moor and to enjoy local pursuits such as riding, fishing, shooting or hunting. Footpaths and bridleways criss-cross the moors, which are abundant with wildlife including red deer, otters and owls.

Along the upper reaches of the River Exe and in the centre of Exmoor National Park, two and a half miles west of Exford, **Westermill Cottages** are a series of charming and comfortable traditional Scandinavian log cottages available for self-catering accommodation. Set amid a 500-acre working farm, this site has won a David Bellamy Gold Conservation Award. there are seven self-catering units in all. "Whortleberry", "Holly", "Gorse", "Bracken", "Ling" and "Molinia" are the names given these characterful cottages. The first three are original

**Westermill Cottages, Westermill Farm, Exford, Minehead,
Somerset TA24 7NJ Tel: 01643 831238
Fax: 01643 831660 e-mail: holidays@westermill-exmoor.co.uk
website: www.exmoor-holidays.co.uk/westermillfarm.htm**

Scandinavian log cottages, while the latter three have been rebuilt to the highest standards. Each is cosy and comfortable, and features a pine kitchen with complete fitted units, electric cooker, fridge, steel sink and drainer, all necessary crockery, pans and utensils, pine furnishings, shower, W.C. and washbasin. Natural spring water comes direct from the farm spring. Sleeping between two and eight people, all have garden furniture that can be used on the raised verandah or grassy area outside. Children are welcome and can play in the sheltered grass paddocks. Some have facilities that make them suitable for people with disabilities. For the family pet, there is a special dog-exercising field by a small stream. All these features offer guests a true rural retreat amid tranquil and supremely comfortable surroundings.

## WHEDDON CROSS
MAP 1 REF B4
7 miles SW of Minehead off the A396/B3224

In the lovely Snowdrop Valley amidst forest woodland, yet just five miles from Dunster and seven miles from the coast, **Ford Farm** is home to the lovely Mill Cottage. An ideal base for exploring Exmoor, this attractive self-catering cottage

**Ford Farm, Wheddon Cross, Minehead,
Somerset TA24 7EE Tel/Fax: 01643 841251**

is set in its own courtyard. Comfortably furnished, this charming cottage offers a
ground-floor lobby with washer/dryer, separate WC and hand basin, well-fitted
kitchen with microwave and electric cooker, and bedroom with two full-size
bunk beds. Upstairs is a double bedroom and a further twin room. Each of these
rooms has its own separate bath. Water is supplied by a natural spring. Carpeted
in snowdrops in February, spring sees the surrounding countryside covered with
primroses followed by bluebells and the scent of wild garlic. In summer the
hedgerows are bursting with wildflowers, while in autumn the fields glow with
colour. Beautiful way-marked walks lead to the moor, where red deer abound.
With many local sights and attractions, this peaceful rural haven makes for a
truly relaxing and comfortable short or long holiday. Well-behaved dogs welcome. Stables available.

WINSFORD                                        MAP 1 REF B5
10 miles SW of Minehead off the B3223

**Karslake House** offers quality accommodation and dining for discerning visitors to Exmoor National Park and the surrounding Somerset countryside. The
house is named after Sir John Burgess Karslake, an eminent lawyer of his day who
was born in 1821 and later became Attorney General and then an MP. This
excellent guest house and restaurant has six superb guest bedrooms, four of which
are en suite while the other two have showers, each one individually furnished
and decorated to a high standard of taste and quality. Spacious and welcoming,
the atmosphere is of a quiet country house, peaceful and relaxing. The elegant

restaurant is open to non-residents, and features an innovative menu of delicious dishes such as roasted salmon fillets, rack of lamb or confit of duckling, all expertly prepared and presented. The wine list is impressive, as is the choice of mouth-watering desserts. Owners Nick and

**Karslake House, Winsford, Exmoor National Park, Somerset TA24 7JE Tel/Fax: 01643 851242**

Juliette Mountford take pride in providing their guests with conscientious service and a genuinely warm welcome. For a taste of luxury amid a delightfully informal and homely ambience, look no further.

## DULVERTON
MAP 1 REF B5
12 miles S of Minehead off the B3223/A396

Set in the centre of Dulverton in the heart of Exmoor, **Page House** is a charming and spacious cottage offering self-catering accommodation. Dulverton is a lovely

village surrounded by wonderful countryside and has a very good local village store, great pubs and a couple of small but impressive restaurants. It is of course also within reach of Dunster, Exmoor and Tarr Steps, as well as acres of beautiful open moorland. The cottage boasts four bedrooms (three doubles and one

**Page House, 12 Lady Street, Dulverton, Somerset Tel/Fax: 01963 250237**

twin), two bathrooms (one with shower), beautifully furnished cottage-style lounge, dining room with open fires if needed, and fully fitted kitchen. It can accommodate up to eight people. The stone and slate house dates back to the 18th century. On the pleasant courtyard, tables and chairs are laid out; there's also a lovely walled garden and small barbecue. Owners Peter and Sheena Doggrell are welcoming hosts who make every effort to ensure that guests staying at the cottage have a pleasant and relaxing stay.

## EXEBRIDGE
14 miles S of Minehead off the A396

MAP 1 REF C6

**Higher Langridge** is a 17th-century farmhouse set amid a working sheep and beef farm overlooking its own peaceful valley. The three guest bedrooms offer superb countryside views; it's not unusual to catch sight of Exmoor's famous Red Deer and other wildlife in the area. The very large and spacious guests' lounge enhances the home-from-home atmosphere, with its log-burning stove, comfortable furnishings and attractive decor. A friendly family ambience pervades this marvellous bed and breakfast. Owner Gill Summers offers all her guests a warm and genuine welcome, and is a conscientious and considerate host. Breakfast is hearty and delicious; evening meals are available by prior arrangement. Both meals make use of fresh local produce, including (for dinner) Exmoor lamb and local trout. Walking, riding, touring

**Higher Langridge Farm, Exebridge, Dulverton, Somerset TA22 9RR Tel/Fax: 01398 323999 e-mail: gill.langridge@ukf.net**

and fishing are all available within easy reach of this charming B & B. Open all year. No smoking.

# TOURIST INFORMATION CENTRES

Locations in **bold** type are open throughout the year

## Bath
Abbey Chambers, Abbey Church Yard, Bath  BA1 1LY
Tel: 01225 477101  Fax: 01225 477787

## Bristol
The Annexe, Deanery Road, Bristol BS1 5DB
Tel: 0117 926 0767  Fax: 0117 9297703
email: bristol@tourism.bristol.gov.uk
website: www.tourism.bristol.gov.uk

## Chard
The Guildhall, Fore Street, Chard  TA20 1PP
Tel/Fax: 01460 67463

## Exmoor National Park
Exmoor House, Dulverton  TA22 9HL
Tel: 01398 323665  Fax: 01398 323150

## Gordano
Junction 19/M5, Gordano Service Area, Bristol  BS20 9XG
Tel: 01275 375516  Fax: 01275 373211

## Minehead
17 Friday Street, Minehead  TA24 5UB
Tel: 01643 702624  Fax: 01643 707166

## Podimore
Somerset Visitor Centre, Forte Services (A303), Podimore  BA22 8JG
Tel: 01935 841302  Fax: 01935 841294

### Sedgemoor Services

Somerset Visitor Centre, Sedgemoor Services M5 (South),
nr Axbridge  BS26 2UF  Tel: 01934 750833   Fax: 01934 750755
email: sominfo@msn.com

### Taunton

Paul Street, Taunton  TA1 3XZ
Tel: 01823 336344
Fax: 01823 340308
website: www.tauntondeane.gov.uk/tourism

### Wellington

30 Fore Street, Wellington TA21 8AQ
Tel: 01823 663379  Fax: 01823 667279

### Weston-super-Mare

Visitor Information Centre, Beach Lawns, Weston-super-Mare,
Avon  BS23 1AT
Tel: 01934 888800  Fax: 01934 641741

### Yeovil

Petter's House, Petter's Way, Yeovil, Somerset  BA20 1SH
Tel: 01935 471279 (24 hours)  Fax: 01935 434065
email: tourism@southsomerset.gov.uk
website: www.southsomerset.gov.uk

# INDEX OF TOWNS, VILLAGES AND PLACES OF INTEREST

# INDEX OF PLACES TO STAY, EAT, DRINK & SHOP

# THE HIDDEN PLACES
# ORDER FORM

To order any of our publications just fill in the payment details below and complete the order form *overleaf*. For orders of less than 4 copies please add £1 per book for postage and packing. Orders over 4 copies are P & P free.

## Please Complete Either:

I enclose a cheque for £ ........................ made payable to Travel Publishing Ltd

## Or:

Card No:

Expiry Date:

Signature: ................................................................

NAME: ................................................................

ADDRESS: ................................................................

................................................................

................................................................

POSTCODE: ................................................................

TEL NO: ................................................................

**Please send to:**   Travel Publishing Ltd
7a Apollo House
Calleva Park
Aldermaston
Berks, RG7 8TN
Tel : 0118 981 7777  Fax : 0118 982 0077

# THE HIDDEN PLACES
# ORDER FORM

|  | Price | Quantity | Value |
|---|---|---|---|
| **Regional Titles** | | | |
| Cambridgeshire & Lincolnshire | £7.99 | ........... | ........... |
| Channel Islands | £6.99 | ........... | ........... |
| Cheshire | £7.99 | ........... | ........... |
| Chilterns | £7.99 | ........... | ........... |
| Cornwall | £7.99 | ........... | ........... |
| Derbyshire | £7.99 | ........... | ........... |
| Devon | £7.99 | ........... | ........... |
| Dorset, Hants & Isle of Wight | £7.99 | ........... | ........... |
| Essex | £7.99 | ........... | ........... |
| Gloucestershire & Wiltshire | £7.99 | ........... | ........... |
| Heart of England | £7.99 | ........... | ........... |
| Hereford, Worcs & Shropshire | £7.99 | ........... | ........... |
| Highlands & Islands | £7.99 | ........... | ........... |
| Kent | £7.99 | ........... | ........... |
| Lake District & Cumbria | £7.99 | ........... | ........... |
| Lancashire | £7.99 | ........... | ........... |
| Norfolk | £7.99 | ........... | ........... |
| Northeast Yorkshire | £6.99 | ........... | ........... |
| Northumberland & Durham | £6.99 | ........... | ........... |
| North Wales | £7.99 | ........... | ........... |
| Nottinghamshire | £6.99 | ........... | ........... |
| Potteries | £6.99 | .......... | ........... |
| Somerset | £7.99 | ........... | ........... |
| South Wales | £7.99 | ........... | ........... |
| Suffolk | £7.99 | ........... | ........... |
| Surrey | £6.99 | ........... | ........... |
| Sussex | £7.99 | ........... | ........... |
| Thames Valley | £7.99 | ........... | ........... |
| Warwickshire & West Midlands | £6.99 | ........... | ........... |
| Yorkshire | £7.99 | ........... | ........... |
| **Set of any 5 Regional titles** | £25.00 | ........... | ........... |
| **National Titles** | | | |
| England | £9.99 | ........... | ........... |
| Ireland | £9.99 | ........... | ........... |
| Scotland | £9.99 | ........... | ........... |
| Wales | £8.99 | ........... | ........... |
| **Set of all 4 National titles** | £28.00 | ........... | ........... |
|  | | _____ | _____ |
|  | | _____ | _____ |

*For orders of less than 4 copies please add £1 per book for postage &
packing. Orders over 4 copies P & P free.*

# THE HIDDEN PLACES
# READER COMMENT FORM

The *Hidden Places* research team would like to receive reader's comments on any visitor attractions or places reviewed in the book and also recommendations for suitable entries to be included in the next edition. This will help ensure that the *Hidden Places* series continues to provide its readers with useful information on the more interesting, unusual or unique features of each attraction or place ensuring that their stay in the local area is an enjoyable and stimulating experience.

To provide your comments or recommendations would you please complete the forms below and overleaf as indicated and send to: The Research Department, Travel Publishing Ltd., 7a Apollo House, Calleva Park, Aldermaston, Reading, RG7 8TN.

Your Name:

Your Address:

Your Telephone Number:

Please tick as appropriate:   Comments ☐        Recommendation ☐

Name of *"Hidden Place"*:

Address:

Telephone Number:

Name of Contact:

# THE HIDDEN PLACES
# READER COMMENT FORM

**Comment or Reason for Recommendation:**

..............................................................................................................

..............................................................................................................

..............................................................................................................

..............................................................................................................

..............................................................................................................

..............................................................................................................

..............................................................................................................

..............................................................................................................

..............................................................................................................

..............................................................................................................

..............................................................................................................

..............................................................................................................

# THE HIDDEN PLACES
# READER COMMENT FORM

The *Hidden Places* research team would like to receive reader's comments on any visitor attractions or places reviewed in the book and also recommendations for suitable entries to be included in the next edition. This will help ensure that the *Hidden Places* series continues to provide its readers with useful information on the more interesting, unusual or unique features of each attraction or place ensuring that their stay in the local area is an enjoyable and stimulating experience.

To provide your comments or recommendations would you please complete the forms below and overleaf as indicated and send to: The Research Department, Travel Publishing Ltd., 7a Apollo House, Calleva Park, Aldermaston, Reading, RG7 8TN.

Your Name:

Your Address:

Your Telephone Number:

Please tick as appropriate: Comments ☐     Recommendation ☐

Name of *"Hidden Place"*:

Address:

Telephone Number:

Name of Contact:

# THE HIDDEN PLACES
# READER COMMENT FORM

**Comment or Reason for Recommendation:**

..........................................................................................

..........................................................................................

..........................................................................................

..........................................................................................

..........................................................................................

..........................................................................................

..........................................................................................

..........................................................................................

..........................................................................................

..........................................................................................

..........................................................................................

..........................................................................................

# MAP SECTION

The following pages of maps encompass the main cities, towns and geo-graphical features of Somerset, as well as many of the interesting places featured in the guide. Distances are indicated by the use of scale bars located below each of the maps

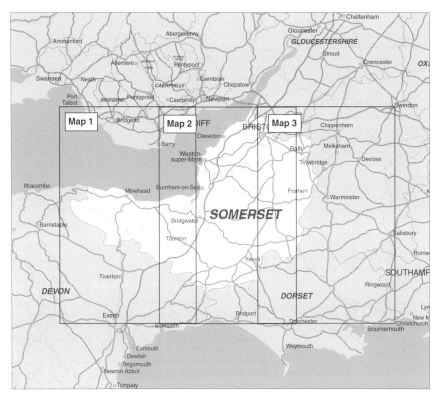

*This page is left intentionally blank*

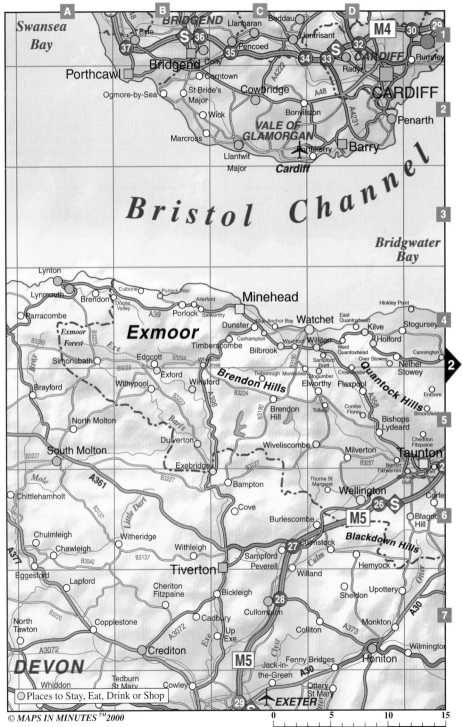

Map 1

# Map 2

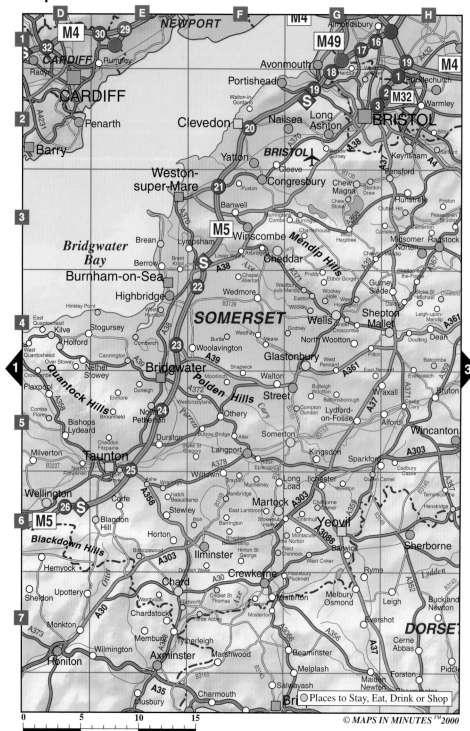

**D** **E** **F** **G** **H**

**1** M4 30 29 *NEWPORT* M4 Almondsbury

32 CARDIFF Rummey M49 16
Radyr 17
CARDIFF Avonmouth 18 Henbury Weston- 19 M4
Portishead 19 on-Trym M32
**2** Penarth S Nailsea Long 2 Warmley
Clevedon 20 Ashton 3 BRISTOL
Barry Yatton *BRISTOL* Barrow Keynsham Saltford
Gurney Bitton
Weston- Cleve Congresbury A38 Pensford
**super-Mare** 21 Puxton Chew Stanton Hunstrete
Banwell Magna Drew Priston
**3** Chew Clutton Hill Peasedown
Winscombe Burrington/ Charterhouse Stoke St John
M5 Combe Burrington West Cameley Camerton
Brean Lympsham Axbridge Harptree Midsomer Radstock
**Bridgwater** Lower Weare Axbridge *Mendip Hills* Norton
**Bay** Berrow Brent S Cheddar Priddy Chewton Mendip Stratton-on-
Knoll Chapel Ebbor Gorge the-Fosse
**Burnham-on-Sea** 22 Allerton Westbury- Wookey Gurney Stoke St
Highbridge Wedmore sub-Mendip Hole West Slade Michael Coleford
Hinkley Point West Easton Horrington Oakhill Leigh-upon-
Huntspill Wookey Mendip A361
**4** East *SOMERSET* Wells Shepton
Quantoxhead Kilve Stogursey Burtle Godney Mallet Dean
Holford Combwich Westhay Meare North Wootton Croscombe Doulting
West Quantock Hills Woolavington Pilton
Quantoxhead Nether Cannington 23 Glastonbury West Batcombe
Over Stowey Stowey Moorlinch Pennard Evercreech Bruton
Crowcombe Bridgwater Shapwick Walton East Pennard Castle
Flaxpool Durleigh Polden Street Cary
Combe Enmore North Hills Butleigh Wraxall
Florey Broomfield Petherton 24 Othery Wootton Battlesborough Alford Wincanton
**5** Bishops Durston Westonzoyland Compton Lydford- A303
Lydeard Cheddon Dundon on-Fosse Cadbury
Milverton Fitzpaine Butrow Bridge Aller Kingsdon Queen Camel Castle
Norton **Taunton** Stoke St Somerton Sparkford Templecombe
Fitzwarren Gregory Henstridge
Wellington 25 Langport Long Ilchester Yeovilton
Ashe Wrantage Willtown Load Chilthorne Sherborne
**6** Corfe A358 Hatch Muchelney Martock A303 Domer
Blagdon Beauchamp Ilton Stoke sub Tintinhull Yeovil
Hill Stewley East Lambrook Hamdon Montacute Barwick
*Blackdown Hills* Horton Barrington Shepton Little Norton
Hemyock Bishopswood Beauchamp West West Coker Ryme
Ilminster Hinton St Chinnock Melbury
Upottery Chard George Osmond Leigh Buckland
**7** Sheldon Wambrook Dowlish Wake Crewkerne Haselbury Newton
Monkton Chardstock Cricket St Plucknett Misterton Evershot *DORSET*
Membury Thomas Clapton Cerne
Wilmington Tytherleigh Forde Abbey Mosterton Maiden Abbas
Axminster Marshwood Beaminster Newton
Honiton Melplash Forston
Charmouth Salwayash Bri...

Places to Stay, Eat, Drink or Shop

0 5 10 15

© *MAPS IN MINUTES* ™2000

**Map 3**

*This page is left intentionally blank*